SEP 1 1 2001

The BRAND MARKETING BOOK

ᛗᛗ AMERICAN **MARKETING** ASSOCIATION

The BRAND MARKETING BOOK

Creating, Managing, and Extending the Value of Your Brand

Joe Marconi

NTC Business Books

NTC/Contemporary Publishing Group

Library of Congress Cataloging-in-Publication Data

Marconi, Joe.
    The brand marketing book: creating, managing and extending the value of
your brand / Joe Marconi.
        p.   cm. (American Marketing Association)
      Includes bibliographical references (p.   )
      ISBN 0-8442-2257-7
      1. Brand name products—Marketing.   I. Title.
HD69.B7M373   1999
658.8′27—dc21   99-23371
                                                      CIP

Some of the material in this book appears previously under the title *Beyond Branding*, published by Probus Publishing/McGraw Hill in 1993.

Interior design by Point West, Inc.

Published by NTC Business Books (in conjunction with the American Marketing
Association)
A division of NTC/Contemporary Publishing Group, Inc.
4255 West Touhy Avenue, Lincolnwood (Chicago), Illinois 60712-1975 U.S.A.
Printed in the United States of America
International Standard Book Number: 0-8442-2257-7
99 00 01 02 03 04 LB 21 20 19 18 17 16 15 14 13 12 11 10 9 8 7 6 5 4 3 2

For Todd and Kristin and Emily,
and for Karin

Contents

Acknowledgments

Thanks to Francesca Van Gorp, Jamie Born, and the staff of the American Marketing Association; to John Nolan, Danielle Egan-Miller, Susan Moore-Kruse, and Denise Betts at NTC/Contemporary Publishing for making our fourth project together a very satisfying one; and to Lonny Bernardi and Rich Girod, and especially to Karin Gottschalk Marconi for just about everything.

Introduction

The baby's smile was "a Kodak moment." The corporation's annual meeting was "a Maalox moment." "Brands," as Kodak also so beautifully put it, "are helping to define the times of our lives."

Marketers have understood that the *brand*—whether considered in terms of brand name, brand equity, or brand loyalty—has been a manageable force in business for decades.

A well-respected marketing professional was heard to say, "People don't buy brands, they buy products. Keep the focus on the *product*." That's a good line—and certainly quotable—but like so much else in the way of quotable business lines, it's a bit too simplistic.

Certainly, people buy products, but *which* products they buy and how they make their buying decisions have a lot to do with how they feel about the brand. Some very successful companies allocate huge budgets for advertising, promotions, and publicity each year. They allocate these budgets in order to become better known, because it is increasingly more accepted among marketers that, in the minds of consumers, a *better-known* brand is thought to be a *better* brand.

Think of the best names in the business—any business. How did they get to be the best names? Imagination, innovation, quality, and style had a lot to do with it. But considerable energy was devoted to defining *what* people think of the brand and *how* people think of the brand.

How important is brand image?

Very important. It is what people remember, if they remember anything at all.

Sometimes brands truly do permeate and become so familiar that they become synonymous with their product category to the point of appearing generic. Coke, Kleenex, and Xerox are constantly battling to protect their trademarks and to make the distinction that they are not categories but *brands*.

It is important to understand the intrinsic value in the brand name. Harvard is regarded as one of the world's greatest universities, but when it allows its name to be used on a repackaged multivolume set of great books (*The Harvard Classics*), or on sweatshirts sold in airport gift shops and department stores, or on a nationally distributed humor magazine, it is using, selling, or exploiting the commercial value of its name—its brand name.

Despite the extremely high failure rate, a rush of new products hits the market each year. Many of them have familiar names: Starbucks, the premium coffee shops that became popular among yuppies in the 1980s, launched an ice cream line that is sold in supermarkets alongside Starbucks Frappuccino bottled beverages. Reese's peanut butter cups, long one of the United States' top-selling candy treats, brought out several candy bar extensions, as well as cookies, breakfast cereal, and jars of its own branded peanut butter; and Virgin Airways, having already moved into the music business with Virgin Records, opened a chain of Virgin Megastores for music, books, and clothing, and even Virgin cola.

Since the early 1990s, as mergers, acquisitions, spinoffs, licensing, and positioning have occupied more attention at both the highest and the lowest corporate levels, the image and the presentation of the brand have become major concerns. Corporate identity and diversification programs have become more sophisticated. The brand and the opportunities inherent in it are often the very basis of product or corporate marketing.

A brand is a name. Brand equity is the value of that name.

While this book is aimed primarily at marketers, the material presented can be useful to CEOs, corporate boards, managers, consultants, and market research personnel at every level.

Consider first the role of the marketer in relating to the brand. Marketers were once regarded as those individuals concerned primarily with pricing and distribution. Marketing professionals today bridge the gap between high-tech and personal service, relying heavily on research, publicity, and advertising. A well-conceived marketing plan will consider graphics, packaging, and positioning. A defined strategy should inform the marketer in all these areas.

Marketing is also a major factor in product development, both initially and for any possible brand extensions.

A marketer must know what the public wants. This may seem like a rather sweeping statement—and it is. In the highly competitive environment of the twenty-first century, anything less will not be sufficient.

- Are a brand's products and services, no matter how successful, meeting the fullest possible range of needs? If not, what can brand managers do about it?

- Is it time for something *new and improved*? A companion product? A whole new line? Perhaps what's needed is new packaging or a flashy (or *less* flashy) new logo.

- What is your "good name" worth to dealers, consumers, merchandisers, franchisers, or franchisees?

- What about prospects for shifting gears entirely, such as taking your business name into an entirely new field?

Billions of dollars are invested in building brands and the suggestion of quality and value that goes with them. Sometimes companies are sold and the original flagship products quickly abandoned. But the valued company *name* or *brand* was what the buyer wanted.

Clearly, time and tastes change. To stay alive, it is sometimes necessary for a company to diversify. When diversification is the best approach, is it better to buy or to build? That decision could depend on a number of considerations. For example, how might a health-conscious public feel about tobacco companies owning food companies and putting their well-known brand names on the label? R. J. Reynolds and Philip Morris encountered just such a problem. Better to buy the companies and retain less controversial names like Nabisco and Kraft on product packaging.

Would moviegoers be comfortable going to see a family film from Seagram's Pictures? Or take the kids to a theme park called Seagram'sLand? Good business sense prompted Seagram's management, after purchasing the MCA entertainment conglomerate (parks, stores, publishers, and movie companies), to stick with the name Universal Studios.

The most astute multinational companies take careful note of psychographic impressions. Mitsubishi works well on a name plate for airplane engines and automobiles, but for a beer...just call it Kirin. Yamaha, on the other hand, worked hard at building equal respect for its brand of motorcycles and pianos. The cost was an investment to address issues of quality and marketing for both product categories, having a great deal of patience, and enormous advertising budgets.

This book will look at names, logos, corporate identity programs, franchising, mergers, name changes, and, perhaps most important, brand building and developing extensions of the brand. It will examine vanity and practicality and consider why the Coca-Cola Company found greater success in its Diet Coke brand than it was able to achieve with Tab. And why, speaking of brand extensions,

Trump Airlines never caused sleepless nights among United Airlines executives.

A design firm president noted that the incredible costs of introducing new brands highlights the need to piggyback on what already exists. The significantly high number of new product failures suggests that a new product bearing the name of an established old favorite increases its odds at achieving acceptance, at least at the trial stage. In a competitive environment, whether the name is old or new, marketers need to understand the importance of creating, managing, and maximizing the impact of a brand in the marketplace. The question of how to do it is what this book will explore.

SECTION 1

*Equity,
Loyalty,
and a
Good
Brand
Name*

1

The Right Name Is a Good Way to Start

"What's in a name? that which we call a rose
By any other name would smell as sweet."
—*William Shakespeare,*
Romeo and Juliet (1595)

"With a name like yours, you might be
any shape, almost."
—*Lewis Carroll,*
Through the Looking Glass (1872)

How much extra might someone pay for a shirt with a leading sports team insignia? Or for a leather jacket bearing the Harley-Davidson logo? Or for T-shirts with the call letters of a favorite radio station? As if proof of the experiment, the NBC Shop (gift and merchandise shops the TV network operates in several major U.S. cities) learned that a shirt or jacket sold for considerably more with the network's logo on it than without.

Why?

Because people want to associate themselves with the images of things they like—and they'll pay extra to do it.

People are also preconditioned to believe that an item with a Nike, DKNY, Mercedes-Benz, or Polo insignia identifies them as being of a particular, very discriminating class.

What's in a name? If the name is Playboy, Xerox, Microsoft, or Barbie, the answer can be counted in millions of dollars.

Once the *idea* of a product or service turns into the actual product or service, the next major issue becomes choosing the right name. Having the right name can be as important as having the right product.

Some brand names are so powerful that they become the generic names of their product categories. We say "Coke" and "Kleenex" and "Xerox" when referring, respectively, to any cola beverage, facial tissue, or photocopy.

Most products, however, have to work hard to be noticed at all, much less to stand out from the pack. Over the years, the approaches to achieving name recognition have been varied, from companies poking fun at themselves ("With a name like Smuckers, it's got to be good") to actually spelling it out for you ("How do you spell relief? R-O-L-A-I-D-S"). Others set their names to music you'll remember. Some name themselves after your town, your state, or someone you love and respect or admire—New York Life, Illinois Tool Works, Mother's Cookies, and Lincoln Savings are a few examples.

Charles Schwab, perhaps America's best-known and most successful discount stockbroker, reportedly said that two of the smartest moves he ever made were putting his name on the company and his picture in his ads. The theory was that people wanted to know the names and faces of people to whom they would be entrusting their money. The name, the face, and the focus of the ad campaign was to suggest integrity and trustworthiness. It helped, of course, that the Schwab name was simple and easy to say and that he was a pleasant-looking, photogenic man. After Mr. Schwab named his "brand" for himself, however, he then had to build it to prominence.

Adman Harry Beckwith, in his book *Selling the Invisible*, wrote, "It's tempting to create a clever name . . . (like) Hair

Apparent for a hair transplant clinic. . . . Don't get funny with your name."

As a general rule that's pretty good advice. Creative people enjoy demonstrating their creativity and believe that nothing less is expected of them, so we get For Eyes as the name of the chain of eyeglass stores or, as on the TV comedy show *Ellen,* a bookshop called Buy the Book. A Chicago store for books and gifts is actually called He Who Eats Mud, clearly one of the more colorful entries in the clever name derby. There's nothing wrong with wanting to be a bit more original than "Bob's Gift Shop," but the key to how far to go with unusual, funny, or clever names is to ask what will generate the most effective, positive response from clients, customers, and prospects. If the name of your business is silly, will it help or hurt business? Despite scoring high in taste tests, the snack food Screaming Yellow Zonkers never quite reached the sales levels of Cracker Jack.

Magazines with names like *Marie Claire, Jane, George,* and *Frank,* which were launched in the 1990s, may make their editors smile, but will they convince an unknowing person standing at an airport newsstand that this is a magazine he or she would like to read? Nobody ever had to wonder what *Car and Driver, Sports Illustrated, House and Garden,* or *Business Week* were trying to say.

Again, to quote Harry Beckwith, "To stand out, stand out. . . . Just as sophisticated marketers do not want their brand names to become generic, you do not want a generic name as your brand."

But between funny names and generic names lie a great many possibilities.

A case of instant brand building occurred when actor Paul Newman put his name and face on jars of Newman's Own salad dressings, sauces, and salsa and containers of popcorn and ice cream. Practically overnight the brand drew attention and recognition. Because of the high quality and excellent distribution of the brand, it gained a very respectable market share for many of its products.

Helen of Troy hair care appliances posted a sales increase some twelvefold over little more than a decade after adding the name of trend-setting hair stylist Vidal Sassoon to its packaging. The reputation of Sassoon immediately became the reputation of the hair dryers and curling irons by virtue of their association with him.

Another instant brand success was the on-line magazine *Salon*. In 1998, as President Bill Clinton's personal relationships became the stuff of congressional hearings and tabloid headlines, the electronic publication broke several important stories that were picked up and led print and broadcast news for days after. Even though only a small percentage of people checked the Internet for their news, all mainstream media and millions of citizens were talking about "that story in *Salon*," and the publication had immediate worldwide recognition and credibility on a par with the major national daily newspapers and TV networks.

Not every new business start-up or young company is going to have a Paul Newman, a Vidal Sassoon, or a breaking news story associated with it. To achieve an identity in the marketplace, the selection of a company name and a product name should be treated as critical decisions. Here are some important considerations in choosing a name:

- Your company name should suggest stability and integrity.

- Your product name, when possible, should say something about the product. Some examples are Fix-O-Dent denture adhesive, Jiffy Lube auto service, or Golden Grain Rice.

- Avoid negative imagery or identification in the product name (AYDS weight-loss candy and wafers was an example of an especially unfortunate product name).

- Try to avoid acronyms. For every IBM th
  hundreds of meaningless, forgettable a
  of letters that say nothing about who y
  you do. Sure, you can buy a personal compu
  from IBM, but how many more can you name?
  People want to buy products and services from
  companies with names.

- Historically, products have achieved a high level of
  recognition when named for a person and
  accompanied by a photograph or an illustration of
  that person (real or fictional) on the packaging or in
  the ads. Examples are Ralph Lauren, Tommy Hilfiger,
  Betty Crocker, Mama Celeste, Chef Boy-ar-dee, Buster
  Brown, Uncle Ben's, Peter Pan, or Duncan Hines, to
  name only a few.

- Upbeat and cheerful names historically outdo bland
  names. Health benefits notwithstanding, Cheerios
  have always outsold 40% Bran Flakes and the
  Chevrolet Impala always outsold the same company's
  Biscayne, even though the designs were very similar
  and the latter car's price tag lower.

Essentially, the recommendations when choosing a name include the following: simple is better than complicated; fewer letters are better than much longer names; and light, upbeat names are better than heavy, pretentious names. Try to tell what the product is or does within the name itself; when possible, suggest or state a benefit; and whenever possible, allude to being big, stable, and worthy of the customer's attention and the purchase price.

Some names are chosen to instantly communicate a message and create an impact—names like Brut and Obsession. Consider the difference in both image and market impact between calling a particular perfume Elizabeth Taylor's Perfume and Elizabeth Taylor's Passion.

An interesting idea that was badly executed involves Arby's, the fast-food restaurant chain. Its specialty is roast beef. Roast beef's initials (r.b.) are pronounced "arby." So, it's a clever idea to name the chain Arby's, except that practically no one gets the connection and most consumers are inclined to think that Arby's, like Wendy's or McDonald's, is named for a person instead of for the product being sold. If the public doesn't make the connection or get the idea and the name is viewed as essentially meaningless, it is a missed marketing opportunity—one a brand may have to overcome.

When Your Brand Name Is the Same as That of Your Corporate Parent, Child, or Sibling Brand

Usually, corporate family relationships are beyond the control of the marketing department, yet they frequently pose challenges, problems, and more than an occasional dilemma.

The New York Palace Hotel changed its name from the Helmsley Palace because the parent company's name was the same as that of a woman who was not only closely identified with the property, but also mired in bad publicity. The connection worked against a very highly regarded property.

The mere announcement that Rupert Murdoch had purchased the *Chicago Sun-Times* caused the well-regarded newspaper's circulation to plummet.

For several years, the Nestlé Company was the target of an international boycott because the division of the multinational giant that sold infant formula to third world countries came under severe criticism. As a result, many thousands of people around the world would not purchase or support well-liked, high-quality products and services, including candy bars, hotels, restaurants, and a premium line of frozen foods.

Beatrice Companies added its name as a tag to television commercials, hoping to raise its stock value by emphasizing its ownership of a broadly diversified group of companies from laundry detergents to candy bars to dairy products and more. While investors may or may not have noticed, the public reacted by wondering why it should be impressed that a soap company made candy, or why such an association proved any of the Beatrice companies were any better.

Brand building is making a product, service, or company stand for something, thus creating a positive interest that would make a defined audience buy or support it and keep supporting it against the efforts of competitors.

If identification with a parent company is going to help further that objective, do it. However, if such an identification will be a negative exercise in ego gratification, or if it could cause the target audience or the public at large to react with indifference, marketers of the company, product, or service might be well-advised to choose another approach.

For many years, General Motors, despite design similarity and no attempt to keep corporate parentage a secret, marketed each of its lines of automobiles strictly independent of one another, with separate dealerships, service departments, and ad budgets and distinct product images for each car. Owners of a Chevrolet, Pontiac, Oldsmobile, Buick, or Cadillac would often express open loyalty to their particular brand while showing disdain for the others, even when they found out that several of the lines and models used interchangeable parts.

The owners' choice of car was and is largely a statement of taste and status. A marketing campaign built around the "GM Mark of Excellence" was a rare attempt to wave the corporate flag above that of the brand, impress

GM stockholders, and attract crossover service business. After achieving high recognition, the campaign was abandoned as a large number of recalls of GM cars left the mark of excellence embarrassingly tarnished.

It might be perfectly fine for General Motors to simply say that it has a car for every budget, lifestyle, and market, but the company instead positions its brands to compete with one another, its dealers fiercely undercutting sister car company prices.

Saturn was a late addition to the GM group of companies and originally, unlike the established cars, avoided overt identification with its industry giant parent. Saturn instead was positioned as an independent brand, a strategy that had special appeal to its target market of young upwardly mobile professionals who preferred to see *themselves* as independent.

Reasons to emphasize or exploit parent company, sister company, or divisional relationships are to:

- emphasize "bigness" and suggest stability and dependability;
- hype the value of parent company stock by generating the highest possible awareness; and
- leverage the perceived importance of the separate or combined companies to create greater buying power, shelf space, or category dominance.

Identifying companies with one another, however, is a double-edged sword. "Bigness" raises consumer (as well as retailer and media) expectations. Those trash bags, for example, had better be of a particularly high quality if they are produced by a division of the Mobil Oil Corporation.

The marketplace will immediately pay greater attention to a product that is "new from" a major, well-respected company, but they will quite correctly expect in return for that instant attention a higher quality product or better service than from a totally unfamiliar name.

In an earlier book, *Crisis Marketing: When Bad Things Happen to Good Companies,* Tylenol was offered as an example of a brand that not only survived, but grew stronger following the deaths of several persons who had ingested tainted capsules. Johnson & Johnson, the brand's parent, effectively exploited its reputation for service, quality, and concern for customers. Most everyone seemed willing and eager to exempt from blame a company whose ethics and long-standing reputation for maintaining high standards of quality put it above reproach. A lesser company, with a less-revered reputation, very likely would have been put out of business by the public rejection, if not by the inevitable lawsuits.

Tylenol quite correctly traded on Johnson & Johnson's good name and reputation, using it as a safety net and going on ultimately to win over an even larger share of the market. In this instance, a case of product tampering, the public did not hold the company to blame for the actions of an individual out to do harm at the expense of the company. The company's and the brand's fine history, if anything, generated a level of sympathy and support that likely would not have occurred if the company had *produced* something that put the customer at risk.

A case that contradicts that last statement involves the Ford Motor Company. The Ford Pinto had a serious defect. Upon impact, in addition to the subcompact car sustaining the usual dents and creases, the gas tank exploded and burst into flames. Ford responded quickly, acknowledging the problem, settling damage suits, and discontinuing production of the model. A public relations campaign emphasized the company's good name, its long history of producing affordable quality products by the millions, and its position as a good citizen of the community. Not only did Ford survive, but the company won the admiration, respect, and support of the marketplace by, in 1992, seeming to reverse the trend of American preference for foreign cars by producing the hugely successful Ford Taurus.

Could another company have fared as well?

Maybe. But more likely not. A large company with a history and a reputation, a good name upon which to draw, was miles ahead of a lesser-known competitor in positioning itself to withstand such a crisis. In addition, its response positioned the brand to capitalize on the crisis by noting how it handled the situation, showing concern for its customers and the quality of its products, and thereby added further luster to its already shining brand name.

Advertising has a "halo effect" by which a company or a product can benefit from the glow of another company or product. Note that ads will often include phrases such as "Snickers—from the makers of Milky Way" or "*The Last Don*—from the author of *The Godfather*." These are not brand extensions, but examples of attempts to use the success of one product to sell another wholly distinct one, suggesting that the new entry belongs in the same quality class as the more established name.

This is usually a very effective strategy, requiring merely that the established product and the new product be of comparable quality. It helps, too, if both the new and the established products are in the same product category, reinforcing the public's perception that the company knows what it is doing and is good at what it does.

Without question, Xerox is the preeminent name in copiers. The company's diversification into the financial services business was viewed as a way to position itself against huge gains in market share by Japanese copier companies. In almost every case, the companies that formed Xerox Financial Services were well-performing entities that Xerox acquired.

While for a time the venture proved profitable, one of the questions that continued to haunt Xerox was why the marketplace should assume quality or product knowledge when an ad for Van Kampen Merritt mutual funds carried the legend "A Xerox Financial Services Company." Why should an investor assume that a fine copy-machine manufacturer knew the first thing about managing mutual funds? The answer is that the investor *shouldn't* make such an assumption. While the parent company's name in the ad might suggest the mutual fund had strong financial backing, the identifier was of no real value in establishing Van Kampen Merritt as a first-rate fund company.

Often a corporate parent's name will not appear anywhere in an ad, on labels, or in product literature when the dissimilarity is so great that calling attention to it might seem curious or even embarrassing. One example of this was Coach, the company that manufactures and sells, often through its own fashionable shops, fine leather products. Coach's products are *so* fine that it has achieved a certain amount of snob appeal with its handbags and briefcases, to name two significant profit areas. Under the circumstances, many people were surprised to learn that Coach's parent company was Sara Lee, the Midwestern corporation best known for its cheesecakes and other fine dessert and food products. It is unlikely that a customer would find the company's excellent reputation for its foods much of a selling point for a pricey handbag. Similarly, Sara Lee didn't see much of an advantage in cross-selling, or making its ownership of Coach widely known. The same was true for Sara Lee's ownership of the fashion and accessories line under the Mark Cross label.

The overall rule regarding how parent companies should identify their relationships with their subsidiary companies, and the subsidiary companies with one another, should be based on clear and distinct advantages to both.

Are There Benefits?

Clearly, Tylenol was saved from a disaster of huge proportions by having Johnson & Johnson as its respected parent.

Coach would not benefit at all from having the world know Sara Lee was its parent.

The infant formula problems caused a worldwide boycott that affected all divisions and products of Nestlé, from candy bars to hotels.

General Motors's name on the mailboxes of its five major divisions was a mixed blessing, inviting both passionate brand loyalty and fierce rejection. Saturn's lack of a clear General Motors connection hasn't seemed to have hurt it.

If the benefit is to both the parent company or brand and to the subsidiary, division, or unit's product in the relationship, exploit it, advertise it, and cherish it. If a benefit can't be clearly defined, don't let corporate vanity and ego get in the way of an otherwise effective marketing effort.

Your Brand, the Stock Market, and the Government

When can you ignore the rule that both the parent company and the subsidiary must benefit from your brand marketing? When the goal of the effort is solely to boost the price of the company's stock.

A bakery and a leather goods company might be an unlikely combination in the minds of consumers, but if both are profitable and are under one stock ticker symbol, this is big and important news to securities analysts.

Typically, touting corporate performance is the editorial province of the *Wall Street Journal, Investor's Business Daily,* and leading national business magazines, such as *Business Week, Forbes,* and *Fortune.* However, when the ever-vigilant business press somehow fails to take notice of a company, and its publicity representative doesn't feel that he or she got the attention deserved, these same publications will only too willingly accept paid ads reporting which mutual fund was number one according to various rating services and which company just reported record profits for the 410th consecutive quarter.

In addition, companies that are a long way from being considered household names have taken their stories to television screens. Archer Daniels Midland (ADM), for example, is a major supplier of raw materials to a wide variety of industries while offering the public no branded product of its own. Why then is ADM a major advertiser, with slickly produced TV commercials on all the Sunday morning news shows?

The answer is that these shows have a large audience of people who evaluate and buy stock—brokers, securities analysts, portfolio managers, investment advisers, fund managers, and investors. The programs are also watched by government regulators and members of legislatures, two groups ADM very much wants to please, impress, and influence. Also staring at the screen are the corporate and business types of a caliber ADM might want to recruit one day or whose company it may want to buy.

For at least a couple of these reasons, Merrill Lynch, Dean Witter, American Family Life Assurance Company (AFLAC), and General Electric are frequent Sunday morning TV news and public affairs show advertisers. Pepsi, Coke, Mattel Toys, and Jiffy-Pop popcorn are not; their efforts are directed at the retail consumer level.

In the late 1990s, pharmaceutical companies began advertising prescription drugs for everything from hair-loss treatments and allergy medications to powerful "wonder drugs" that would both lower cholesterol levels and reduce risks of heart attacks. The ads might typically be three-page color layouts in national editions of general-interest magazines such as *Time* and *People*. The same product might be the subject of a television spot.

In both types of advertisement, slice-of-life scenes might show a young couple talking hopefully about their future or grandparents discussing the desire for a rich, full life.

In most instances, children are prominent in the sentimental scene that ends with the words "Ask your doctor." And *do* people actually ask their doctors about these drugs? Has the culture evolved to a point where patients are suggesting to their doctors what prescriptions are to be written?

In some cases, yes. Mostly, though, these ads are aimed at Wall Street as the "next big drug" that has a high degree of brand awareness. Zocor, Mevacor, Viagra, Allegra, Lamisil, Prilosec, Zomig, Zyrtec, Claritin, and Flonase are some of the products available by prescription only, yet they are advertised to the consumer public in large, colorful ads in prominent national general-interest magazines. These ads can suggest to the investment community that a particular drug company is ahead of the curve in developing breakthrough consumer products. They say that this company's stock, if not the company itself, is one for the "watch" list or merits a straight-out "buy" recommendation.

The other audience segment that these ads seek to influence are legislators and regulators who hold the decision-making power over whether a particular drug will make it to market or be readily available. Creating a public demand for a brand is a strategy aimed at getting attention, and government employees, appointees, and elected officials are as susceptible to public opinion as anyone, perhaps more so.

Logos, Signatures, and Acronyms

A logo is typically a symbol, whether commonplace or creative, that is used to stand for a company or product. A signature, as with one's personal signature, is the way in which a company or product name is represented graphically. Some ad historians believe the very concept of brand began with the creation and use of the logo. That symbol, that identifying mark, distinguished one product from another.

For years, some people had to check the plaque or hood ornament on a GM car to tell a Pontiac from an Oldsmobile. They looked virtually alike, except for their logos. Considerable amounts of money are invested in market research to determine what symbols prove to be the strongest, most persuasive elements of influence. They must be pleasing to the eye, memorable, and reflective of the product itself.

The process of creating a unique and distinctive logo often looks so simple, as in the case of General Motors (logo: the letters "GM" encased in a rectangle), General Electric (logo: the letters "GE" in a thin circle), or IBM (logo: the letters "IBM"). Designers and graphic artists will painstakingly explain that the process is much more complex than it appears. Dozens of illustrations and artistic executions are considered before a final selection is made. Countless styles of typeface are evaluated and tested. Indeed, in the case of Xerox (logo: the word "Xerox"), an original typeface was created.

A story destined to become part of corporate identity folklore is NBC's wanting to replace its colorful peacock logo with something more crisp and contemporary. A prestigious design firm was retained. After a fair amount of time, with cost reported to be around $750,000, the network proudly revealed its new symbol, a letter "N." Initial public reaction was a chortle, which then turned into a horse laugh when a small public television station announced that it had been there first, using a nearly identical letter "N" as its logo for some time and, by the way, it had been created for them for a few hundred dollars. The incident might have been enough to set back the very idea of corporate logos. A little more research, a little more creativity, and a little less fanfare could have saved the broadcast giant a lot of embarrassment.

While the basic function of the logo is to identify a product or company and to make it more distinguishable among competitors, psychological influences and impact are significant. Often it is not just a symbol that is involved but *symbolism*. The Dreyfus lion and the Merrill Lynch bull are two examples of attempts to infer power, strength, and dominance among peers, together with a suggestion of animal magnetism. The target audience is supposed to get all this from a symbol before the product name is revealed.

But that is the *essence* of the logo concept. When it succeeds, it identifies something without saying or showing its name. While it is true that some companies use a very distinctive typeface and design as their logo, others prefer to tell you who you are watching or dealing with by sign, not syllable:

- Golden arches say McDonald's
- A rock means Prudential
- An eye suggests CBS
- A winged horse identifies TriStar Pictures
- A winged shoe identifies Goodyear
- A torch on a shield says Amoco
- A "T" in a star in a circle is Texaco
- A little girl, holding an umbrella, walking in the rain, means Morton Salt

These companies have done such an effective job of permeating people's consciousness that their symbols (especially on common items, such as caps, jackets, mugs, canvas bags, pens, key rings, or other promotional devices) cause one to immediately think of the company or product. The continued visibility over time is critical. Note that many of the most successful brand names in their respective businesses have had the same logo for a very long time. Companies that frequently change their corporate identity programs are ones that seem to have a difficult time establishing themselves in the public's mind.

Some companies seem to have it easy when it comes to creating or adopting a logo. Unfortunately, not all companies have visual names like Green Giant, Birdseye, or Arm & Hammer. Logos, however, will often change to reflect fashion trends. The marketplace will at first appear to be awash in a sea of arcs, swirls, and waves; as the cycle changes, these logos are often replaced by the company name in a simple, understated typeface. Columbia Records, Chrysler, and RCA are companies that have an almost predictable cycle of understated-to-overstated-and-back-again corporate graphics.

Acronyms identifying a company or product by the first letters of its name are a kind of visual and verbal shorthand that presumes the marketplace knows a company by its name, initials, or both. If the marketplace guesses wrong, the product's (or company's) identity suffers, perhaps twice. If the company succeeds, of course, one might say they are twice as well known.

These are some products or companies as well known by their initials as they are by name, sometimes better:

AAA	GMAC	MCI
A&P	GTE	MGM
AT&T	IBM	NCR
A&W	IDS	RCA
BASF	ITT	STP
BMW	JVC	TNT
GAF	KFC	TRW
GE	KLM	TWA
GM	MCA	

Al Ries and Jack Trout in their book *Positioning: The Battle for Your Mind* discourage the use of corporate or product acronyms, a process they refer to as "the no-name trap."

They note also that a number of companies "go to a lot of trouble making sure [their] name looks right without considering how it sounds." True enough. People are sensitive to both sight and sound. Your name, logo, and signature, on items from products to ads to trucks and balloons, should both look and sound right. We will easily call one city L.A., but another is never called N.Y. It just doesn't sound right. A form of corporate shorthand is fine for internal memos and reports, but the best way to let people know and become familiar with a company or product name is to *use* that name as much as possible.

Corporate Identity Programs

In many respects, a corporate identity program is like a dress code—defined, inflexible, and rich in symbolism. Some companies, like individuals, take great pride in their name and do not grant others the right to shorten, change, or misuse it. Just as some men named Robert prefer not to be called Bob, businesses go to great lengths to protect and control the use of their names. The premise, of course, is totally legitimate and honorable, particularly in instances where a great investment has been made in research, focus groups, graphics arts, and advertising. Editorially, total control is practically impossible.

No matter how much the company may wish it to be so, AT&T can never stop reporters from referring to it as Ma Bell, and Howard Johnson's Motor Lodge can't seem to keep many people from calling it HoJo.

When it comes to companies themselves, they can and do exercise control over their various divisions, advertising agencies, public relations agencies, or anyone else wishing to use their trademarked name in signage, an endorsement, or another form. Usually this is quite appropriate. Such requirements as indicating trademark, registration, patent, or copyright are correct.

To insist that a name be used as intended—not hyphenated, broken, or modified—is certainly appropriate. Many companies, having invested heavily in establishing corporate colors, may require that when a logo or signature is represented in color, it be in the designated PMS or corporate color. It is even understandable to insist that when a logo is used among other logos, a particular placement or position requirement be adhered to and a size relationship of one logo to another be maintained. If Coca-Cola's logo were to be shown in the same space as Pepsi, or Hilton along with Hyatt, the companies would reserve the right not to be upstaged by their competitors.

An appropriate checklist for the correct use of a company's corporate identity symbols (its logo and signature) could probably be represented in a page or two. Many companies have invested large sums of money on corporate identity programs and apparently believe they haven't gotten their money's worth if they don't have a thick volume ("The Corporate Identity Manual") to cap it off.

Experience has shown that after determining size, color, placement, and legal requirements, almost all other information in corporate identity manuals is of dubious value, so they don't get used much. Save a tree, save a forest, skip the manual, and keep the requirements for the use of your name simple. Businesses should want the exposure that leads to greater awareness and usage, to brand loyalty and brand equity. Ridiculous and complicated requirements discourage such use.

Name Changes, Mergers, and Joint Ventures

"Change for the sake of change" is a very questionable policy under the best of circumstances. To be honest, ad agencies will often suggest changes to clients, and marketing or ad directors will suggest changes to senior management, whether it's a new logo or a new name or acronym for the company itself, just to keep up with the times. Sometimes, as risky as such a move can be, it is simply motivated by a desire to generate additional billings. Sometimes it is a function of creative people being creative and acknowledging that they are only doing what they do with the brand or company's best interests in mind. But sometimes, a push for change is an attempt to propose something new before management has a chance to get tired of the status quo and sends everyone scrambling.

As a general rule, businesses should not do something without a reason. Sometimes, a stated reason is that management feels the company needs a face-lift or a bit of repositioning within its category so that it has a more contemporary sound, look, and feel about it. After all, it's been years since—

- Wait!!
- Stop and listen to yourself!
- Is your market share holding steady or declining?
- Is your competition wiping your nose in every market?
- How are profits?
- Are customers, retailers, wholesalers, and stockholders satisfied?

Check your research data (or commission more current research) and analyze it carefully.

Too often, a new manager or management team will want to "put their own stamp on things," as the saying goes. That's fine if it stops at rearranging the furniture or changing long-distance phone companies, but for something as dramatic and significant as changing a product or company name—one in which considerable money and a reputation may have been invested—be careful.

The Campbell Soup Company had what many people might have considered the same, familiar, basic, unexciting red and white label on its cans for years. The company also had about two-thirds of the estimated $2.3 billion canned soup market. The name and logo were largely the same as they had been and were even immortalized as a pop-culture icon in a famous painting by artist Andy Warhol. As new varieties of soup were introduced, consumers sometimes had to squint to find the snip with the word *new* on the label. But it was worth it. The public had put its trust in the brand over the years, taking its quality and consistency as a given, and if one day the labels were gold and blue, the well-earned familiarity would be gone and confidence in the product would be questioned. Such a change would be unnecessary and an example of change for the sake of change.

The company did achieve an element of freshness by incorporating small photos of particular vegetables on the cans' labels—subtle visual representations of the types of soups that were in the cans. For a time, the company even incorporated small photographs of the members of the champion Women's U.S. Olympic Figure Skating Team onto the labels. Campbell Soup was a sponsor of the team and wanted to capitalize on its popularity. But, whether skaters or vegetables, the photographic art was incorporated simply and tastefully, not intruding in any way on the familiarity of the famous red and white label. A more radical change would have been unnecessary and very unwise.

Canned soup, like anything else in business, will experience ebbs and flows according to weather, lifestyle, and its fashionability at any given time. However the business may fluctuate, Campbell Soup has not lost it to a competitor.

Do some research and act on its findings. If it tells you that you're doing fine and what you are doing is working well, say thank you and get back to work. New managers, new marketers, or a new ad agency should have an arsenal of creative weapons available to *maintain* that fresh, competitive energy. Allow the creative marketers to do their jobs, but don't allow them to fix something that isn't broken.

Be suspicious of people who want to "shake things up" for no reason other than that the expression sounds good to them. This style of management exists, though no one seems to be able to explain why. Remember that just because a new CEO or marketing chief doesn't like a name doesn't mean it is a bad name. Check the results of the research to confirm or disprove opinions before taking action that can set back a brand and create a competitively perilous situation.

Sometimes, of course, the need for change is so obvious that it doesn't need research to reveal it. It may or may not have anything to do with your brand. The public's tastes change; particular products or locations become less popular; certain products (such as tobacco, fur, fried foods) generally fall from favor. Whatever circumstances motivate it, action is called for.

At one time S. S. Kresge, like its chief competitor F. W. Woolworth, was doing just fine with its chain of neighborhood five-and-ten stores. But when Kresge's married the idea of the supermarket to that of the discount department store, with shopping carts, product sampling, instant in-store sales, and specials on products from coats to tires to candy canes, plus plenty of free parking, business exploded. Thus Kmart was born, becoming so successful that ultimately the parent took the child's name and all of Kresge became Kmart. The concept was sound and the Kmart brand name distinguished it, giving it a unique strong identity it could not have projected under the Kresge banner, given the image associated with that name.

When Nash became American Motors, sales continued to fall. The company next tried changing its name to that of its most successful product, Rambler, but sales still lagged. The cars simply were not good enough to compete, regardless of their names or the company that made them. Occasionally even the brightest marketers are reminded that, whatever the name of the brand or how good the advertising, it still takes a good *product* to succeed.

Market research told Montgomery Ward department stores that stereo systems, computers, and other electronic equipment, such as answering machines, videocassette recorders, and portable phones, were being increasingly purchased by younger people. Further, these younger customers wanted the most technically advanced products available. The same research indicated that customers believed the best quality, price, and selection were to be found at electronics specialty stores, not at department stores where their parents bought furniture, clothing, lawn mowers, and so on. Wards's response was to create a store-within-a-store, Electric Avenue.

With its own identity, budget, and ad campaign, the venture was a huge success. Many ads for Electric Avenue gave a location, but never mentioned it was within or attached to a Montgomery Ward store. Further, Electric Avenue maintained a hot, youthful image that was very different from the image of Montgomery Ward, the middle-class, mainstream department store that gave it birth. A residual benefit to the parent was that younger shoppers gave Wards a second look. The company was appealing to a younger market, without alienating its older, core customers. Ultimately, Electric Avenue would have to struggle to have it both ways—to be perceived as an aggressive competitor of electronic specialty stores while also essentially remaining the electronics department of a large department store. The store-within-a-store, having essentially a brand-within-a-brand, is a solid concept that can work.

In another example, a giant Japanese automaker had global marketing reasons for changing the name of its popular Datsun to Nissan. The transition went smoothly because it was a nondomestic company. While the American car buyer had a certain level of familiarity with the

Datsun brand, there were also a growing number of foreign companies entering the market. To take a closer look at Nissan amid the many other new imports didn't seem too much to ask. An American automaker attempting the same type of brand name change would have had to go considerably further—say, if Ford decided to change the name of its Mercury division to that of another planet. Established American brands take on an institutional quality that few foreign companies can claim in the U.S. market.

AYDS weight-reducing candies and wafers came on the market and were selling pretty well a generation before the tragic and fatal acquired immune deficiency syndrome (AIDS, as it was more commonly called by medical researchers) became the modern equivalent of the plague. A new name and a reintroduction of the diet product certainly was in order. Instead, the manufacturer stopped advertising the brand and allowed it to languish quietly for a time and then disappear.

Sometimes, after a name change has been decided, there is a tendency to want to put "formerly..." under the new name. Let it go. Focus on now and the future.

Merging companies represent a unique challenge. Which name goes first? Regardless of which entity might be larger, which brand or name is more popular? Do you resolve the matter by selecting a neutral new name and in the process risk losing a measure of the loyalty, prestige, or brand equity that either or both of the merging entities may have had?

If the names fit comfortably together, use them with a slash, hyphen, comma, or space between them. Resolve the matter of who goes first by putting the larger, better-known brand name first, unless that combination creates a look and sound that is not pleasing. If agreement can't be reached, settle on a neutral name and commission a terrific ad campaign to make sure that everyone knows about it. Such a campaign should present your message without insulting your constituency. For example, when

Illinois Bell Telephone company changed its name, as part of the government-dictated breakup of the old Bell System, billboards and full-page ads appeared with the message "We asked you what you wanted in a phone company and we've changed our name to Ameritech."

Huh?

Without having reviewed the actual research to determine if customers were asked what they wanted in a phone company, it is probably safe to conclude that an overwhelming number of persons responding would *not* have answered, "Change your name to Ameritech." This was a vanity ad message that had nothing to do with the customer, an approach that is always wrong.

Sometimes in mergers and acquisitions, decisions are dictated by the dreaded legal department. As egos and golden parachutes begin to unfurl, remember that all the rules for naming the product or company still apply. If your research tells you that consumers, retailers, and stockholders like it, it's good. If the name is a vanity decision, it's bad—and could end up being very expensive.

When Chrysler Corporation took over the failing American Motors, the latter company was in such sad shape that there was little point in keeping the name alive. As its troubles mounted, American Motors was a major news story for months, and to keep the name in front of the public would only perpetuate its negative image. The company's few popular models (the Jeep and Eagle brands) were simply brought out during the next model year as products of Chrysler.

The pairing of the two very respected Hollywood logos for Metro-Goldwyn-Mayer and United Artists by their common corporate owner resulted in MGM-UA, a lackluster name that failed to capitalize on the illustrious history or public affection associated with both companies' brands.

The rule of joint ventures is that there are no rules. Normally, including the line "A joint venture of . . ." allows the opportunity to capitalize on whatever goodwill, awareness, or positive reputation the venture's partners may have had individually. The suggestion is of strength through combining the component parts, without the loss of positive qualities associated with either or both.

Recognize the power and value that comes with having the right name for your brand. It is the identifier that, upon immediate sight or sound, will often remind people how they feel about the brand forever.

Choose a name or change to a name that distinguishes you from the pack in the most favorable possible way. In an ad-heavy, information-heavy environment, few choices you make will tell your public so much or carry such currency over time as your brand name. Choose carefully.

Protecting Your Brand Name

The choice is important and making the *wrong* choice could hurt the product's chances for success, but sometimes the process can be unexpectedly costly if your plans are stalled, altered, or halted because of a contested name. Every year the courts hear cases of name and trademark infringement. These cases are often brought by, and defended by, some of America's largest and most distinguished corporations, folks that seem so big and thorough as to be above all that.

It is as important to legally protect a name as it is to create one. Henri Charmasson, a consultant in such matters, offers the following:

> A good name to identify a company or distinguish its products from others must be unique and original, yet capable of carrying a favorable message to motivate the customer to have dealings with that company. Creating such a name is an art as well as a science with rules and guidelines rooted in

sociology, psychology, semantics, and last but not least, the law.

Commercial names such as *Super Glue* for an adhesive, *Reader* for a newspaper, *Lite* for a low calorie beer and *Windsurfer* for a sailboat . . . are examples of names that courts found to be unworthy of legal protection and have been freely copied as a result.

Some other examples of names that companies tried to own, but that were ruled too generic to register, include *air shuttle* for short-route airline service; *builders emporium* for a building supply store; *computer merchant, computer store,* and *consumer electronics* as the respective purveyors of the items named; *dial-a-ride* for ground surface taxi shuttle service; and *Safari* for an outlet that would carry, not surprisingly, safari gear. Obviously, the limitations of name ownership extend to the services noted. For example, one might trademark *Safari* for a restaurant or nightclub with a special theme or menu and likely be granted exclusivity.

In the case of *The Computer Store,* one can picture an excited marketer thinking how great it would be to have a name that was so obvious and all-encompassing. It would seem like the generic designation of the industry itself. Alas, the courts agreed with that perspective and wouldn't let them have it.

In building a successful brand name, it is important to be distinctive. A generic-sounding name may indeed tell people what you do, but it will not go very far in helping to distinguish or differentiate you from your competition.

Building Your Brand

1. Choose a name for your company, product, service, or association that suggests strength, substantial size,

and stability; has a pleasing look and sound; is not too long, complex, or difficult to remember or to spell; and, most important, suggests what the company or product is or does.

2. Try to show a benefit in your name. *Easy, quick, fresh, safe, rapid, instant,* and *sure* are some examples of words used commonly in brand names to suggest benefits.

3. Let decisions regarding how you represent your relationship to a corporate parent or an associated company be determined by evaluating what benefits accrue to each and how such benefits can be conveyed to customers. If there is no reason to link the entities except to please or impress the board of directors, save describing the association for the annual report. Dislike of a parent company can be passed along to the public as easily as an appreciation.

4. Address different audiences differently. Consumers and retailers want to know about benefits to *them.* Don't burden your public with needless explanations of your trademarks, patents, and corporate parents.

5. Logos and signatures should be memorable and should say something about the company or product. Try to include an element that differentiates it from its competition. Words such as *best, top, just,* and *only* are some that have been used historically in trying to set products apart with a sense of uniqueness and market superiority.

6. Avoid the acronym game; use *names* and *words* to suggest a company or product's pride, spirit, or benefit.

7. Avoid generating volumes on the use of and restrictions on your name and logo. A simple directive on size, colors, placement, and trademark

protection is enough. Don't waste time and money creating a thick corporate identity manual that no one will read.

8. Rely on market research, sales information, and feedback from your customers and constituents to tell you if your name still "works" and has value in the marketplace. If it doesn't, consider a change in any of a number of forms, including a fresh start with a new name, a repositioning of your brand name, a new market niche, or a "new and improved" version of your product or your company.

9. Avoid making changes just to appear fresh and exciting. Be responsive to your market and change only if and when you need to do so.

10. Think of your company name or product name as having every bit as much the suggestion of pride and history as the best family names. Such names are passed on with a great sense of tradition through the generations.

11. Protect your name legally. Name and trademark challenges are costly and result in negative public attention.

12. Avoid adopting generic-sounding names that fail to convey a sense of uniqueness and probably would not successfully withstand a legal challenge from others in your field.

2

Building Equity in
Your Brand

"Nothing is wasted, nothing is in vain:
The seas roll over but the rocks remain."
—*A. P. Herbert,*
Tough at the Top (c. 1949)

"There is less in this than meets the eye."
—*actress Tallulah Bankhead (in 1922)*

A product or service exists and it has a name. The appropriate trademark protections have been secured. The next step is to turn that name into a *brand* by infusing it with distinction and a suggestion of value. What makes a name a brand is that though a name is an identifying designation, the *brand name* is identified with a personality.

Professor John Philip Jones of Syracuse University wrote, "A brand is a product that provides functional benefits plus added values that some customers value enough to buy." Professor David Aaker, however, goes a step and several words further in his definition, suggesting, "A brand is a distinguishing name and/or symbol (such as a logo, trademark, or package design) intended to identify the goods or services of either one seller or a group of sellers, and to differentiate those goods or services from those of competitors."

Whew!

Creating a Brand

While neither of the distinguished professors above is likely to go on to a career as an ad copywriter, the point should be clear that brands are names and symbols of what they represent.

Now that a brand has been brought into existence, the role of the marketer is to bring it into the marketplace and to the attention of known and potentially interested parties. This is done by building equity in a brand, that is, by building the value in and of the brand.

Without making this seem like Marketing 101, consider this rather basic question: Why do people buy?

Whether a purchase is a necessity or simply something the buyer wants, why do people choose the brands that they choose? What are the buyers' *hot buttons*?

The answer looks like this:

$$\frac{\text{Price} + \text{Quality} = \text{Value}}{\text{Image}}$$

Historically, the price/quality/value tag was largely associated with brand names. The drill went like this:

If you were a *better-known* brand in the minds of consumers, you would be considered a *better* brand. You would be better known because you were big and highly visible, because you advertised more, because you had a larger advertising budget, because you had an overall larger operation, because you sold more product. You did this because you were tops: you had a high-quality product that was priced right. Note that priced right doesn't mean *cheapest*. Cheap can be synonymous with shoddy, poor, or of low quality. And price without quality does not equal value. Price *with* quality equals value, and value is why people choose one brand over another.

That and *image*—that "feel good" quality.

When someone buys a Mont Blanc pen or a Lexus automobile, fine wine or good crystal, that person believes that he or she is buying quality at an acceptable (though certainly not the *cheapest* available) price. With it the buyer gets a feeling of taste, style, accomplishment, and, yes, status or, just as important, the perception of status.

Kmart stores offer Martha Stewart Signature Collection towels and sheets or women's clothing from The Jaclyn Smith Collection. These items carrying celebrity names and endorsements promise taste and style at a fraction of the cost of top European or New York designers. Kmart shoppers are buying the celebrity's image.

Image is a major factor in most buying decisions. Often it has to do with the image to which one aspires and the image that fits a certain belief system. A person who believes that no car should cost as much as a house would not buy an expensive luxury car under any circumstances. Many people will never pay the considerable extra cost of flying first class, whether they can afford it or not.

Some people will claim that they bought their particular cars for a host of reasons, from good mileage to economy to resale value. However, the one reason that researchers feel is near the top of the list is *image*. There is a desire to slide behind the wheel and feel, if only for a short time, like James Bond.

But while the perception of price, quality, value, and image has been long identified with established brands, modern marketing techniques and technology are challenging that idea.

The Power of the Media in Brand Building

Technology gets blamed for a lot. In addition to speed and accuracy, the computer has brought us a new list of excuses for things going wrong (or not going at all). "The system's down; We're not programmed for what you want; Our system's not compatible with your system," and, a particular favorite, "We must have a computer virus."

But, for all the excuses, technology has produced a world of instant communication.

Marketers had spent years creating brand identification and recognition and building brand loyalty, only to be dramatically upstaged by instant brand building in the Information Age.

Marketers, visionaries that they are, saw it coming, not only watching but facilitating its evolution:

- In the 1950s, when Arthur Godfrey told his television and radio audiences that he was pausing for a cup of Lipton Tea, America put the kettle on with him and Lipton outsold its competitors, virtually owning the U.S. market.

- When Paul Harvey told his national radio audience about "the Gold Book" from Banker's Life and Casualty Company, Americans did the unthinkable. They actually called and asked to speak to a life insurance salesperson.

- In the 1960s, Dick Clark told the millions of teenagers watching TV's *American Bandstand* that Beechnut Spearmint gum was "flavor-ific," and the product literally sold out coast-to-coast overnight. It became instantly the brand of choice of America's youth.

- The power to rapidly build a brand proved itself when, in the 1980s, the fledgling Apple Computer and the little-known Nike each spent virtually their entire year's advertising budget to run one-minute commercials during the Super Bowl game. These commercials would be talked about for months—

free—on radio and TV talk shows, on subways and commuter trains, and over coffee across America.

- And then there was the appearance by billionaire H. Ross Perot, an unknown figure nationally, who declared his candidacy for the presidency of the United States on cable television's *Larry King Live*. The story was picked up by wire services and transmitted to newsrooms around the world. By the next day, Perot's name was known and he was being regarded as a viable candidate. With a proliferation of cable TV and satellite channels and the Internet, such is the power and capability of modern media technology.

Consumers constantly complain about the glut of advertising: "There's too much of it; it's intrusive, insulting, demeaning, and mindless, especially on television." Yet, when

- Victoria's Secret models made their transition from catalog page to television screen in scenes that reflected the fantasies of most postadolescent boys; and
- models seemingly nude or near-nude and, in any event, gracefully moving as if in a dream ballet appeared in an artfully constructed black-and-white Calvin Klein ad (both TV and print)

people stopped what they were doing time and again and watched. More important, they *bought* the products and sales soared.

The common thread in these examples, of course, is the use of sex appeal—not exactly an original idea in advertising campaigns. The old adage is "sex sells," yet there have also been innumerable ads with sexy models and pitches that have fallen flat. The technology may have provided the medium and the medium provided the audience, but bad advertising still annoys people and usually doesn't work. Sex does not really sell in advertising. Sex *gets the audience's attention,* but making the sale and building the brand takes more than getting attention.

Good advertising works, even amid the glut. A single, well-done TV commercial, seen often, can create a level of interest that establishes a brand permanently.

While McDonald's may long be the fast-food leader, the Golden Arches team had to endure being upstaged by a rival that, although it had been around awhile, became an instant brand success. Wendy's had been considered an OK place for hamburgers and shakes, but not an especially sizzling property. When the company ran a TV spot with an 80-something, foggy-voiced grandmother asking, "Where's the beef?" at a rival burger chain outlet, Wendy's sales soared. The line became a part of pop culture as comedians, editorial writers, and politicians repeated it from coast to coast, each time providing free advertising by conjuring up memories of Wendy's. Later ads went on to feature Wendy's founder, Dave Thomas, a friendly, seemingly good-hearted man, who provided a "brand personality" and positioned the chain as a friendly family place.

Advertising Creates Awareness

There are other ways to generate awareness, certainly some less expensive than television advertising. But when it comes to presenting your message, controlling the timing, space, content, and the number of times and places the messages will be viewed by a scientifically determined demographic target, advertising in general, and TV advertising in particular, does work.

- Advertising creates awareness.
- There is a measurable relationship between level of awareness and share of market.

These proven facts relate directly to the premise offered in the Introduction, that *if you are a better-known brand, you are a better brand.*

Brand equity is the value, or the perception of value, in the brand name. Establishing that value begins with creating awareness. There are two ways to do this: quickly or slowly.

The slow process, which some would argue is more likely to achieve deeper-edged, more lasting results, involves several steps:

1. Going *market by market* or city to city to introduce the product to
   a) test groups
   b) influential persons or groups who will endorse or otherwise raise the level of awareness through word-of-mouth advertising

2. *Sampling*—providing free product samples (or free trial service) to targeted groups on a market-by-market basis.

3. *Advertising*—As a step in the process or as an option, media advertising (print, radio, TV, outdoor) or point-of-sale displays and promotions provide a more traditional approach. What is *not* traditional in the most effective programs and campaigns is the creativity involved in both the media plan and the advertisements themselves.

   "Awareness advertising" lets the public know that the product *exists*; "image advertising" influences how the public *feels* about the product. Either approach can be powerful or memorable with the right creative treatment. The media plan details where, when, and how often the work is presented. It can include safe and proven-effective mainstream placements or unusual outlets that, while riskier, often gain greater attention.

4. *Sponsorships*—The possibilities are just about limitless: TV shows, art exhibits (from fine art to pop art), student competitions, Little League, scholarship grants, concerts, and sporting events from golf or tennis tournaments to car racing and bicycle marathons to the Special Olympics.

5. *Promotions*—an area that has truly come of age. Once this meant putting a company name or logo on pens and key rings. It's still that, plus quality clothing, jewelry, and other brand-identified premiums that both involve the recipient and keep the brand name present and visible in the home or work environment. Promotions are also tie-ins with books, movies, events, and other products and projects that maximize budgets and visibility.

6. *Public relations*—generating awareness through the use of "non-paid" media, such as television and radio interviews and call-in shows; placement of stories, expositions, and announcements.

7. *Event or cause participation*—A little PR and a little sponsorship yield a lot of recognition, visibility, and awareness. Subsidies, endowments, and grants (the support of a school, charity, or another worthy cause) have long been subtle but effective methods of earning recognition, awareness, and brand loyalty by doing good.

8. *Endorsements*—recognition by an independent research or testing organization often separates and distinguishes quality; examples are receiving the *Good Housekeeping* Seal of Approval or being recommended by "9 out of 10 doctors surveyed."

The quick way to achieve brand awareness is to do all of the above listed steps, only more quickly. Critics of this process call it *hype*, and those who undertake it can't be thin-skinned. This kind of campaign makes a very aggressive bid for attention.

While the slower process, step by step and market by market, might be completed over a period of years (a three- to five-year test and phase-in is not unusual), the quick alternative might have a company accomplishing steps one through eight in months or perhaps within a single high-profile event, the impact of which would linger and result in more word-of-mouth advertising. One example of this was the Microsoft launch of its Windows 95 software program, which received saturation coverage on television, radio, all print publications, and news shows, as well as on thousands of World Wide Web sites.

Many brands have benefited over the years from the slow, methodical process of program sponsorship building a star-quality brand:

Mobil Masterpiece Theater

The Bell Telephone Hour

Ford Theater

Hallmark Hall of Fame

Wonderful World of Disney

Kraft Theater

Years ago, the fast-break hype approach was regarded as too flashy and not readily adopted. The slower market-by-market alternative allowed for gauging public response and, if necessary, making adjustments or even major changes before moving on. If a product fared badly in initial markets, it might never see national release. This was a limit-your-losses approach.

It is true that the quicker approach, doing everything at once, costs a lot more than easing your way into a market and paying as you go. The rationale for it, however, is that if you believe you are likely to implement the full program (or something like it) over time, whether the reasons have to do with faith or commitment, there are economies of scale involved in making deals and power buying. Skilled media planners, who know the costs of buying individual, finely targeted markets, can make national and network buys, reaching those same markets for a fraction of the cost-per-market of the local buys. Simply put, a major time or space buy has more price-negotiating leverage and power than a minor local buy.

In addition, there are often enormous research, development, and other start-up costs involved, and investors frequently want quick evidence that a product is on the right track. A big splash tends to get a fairly immediate response. Further, it is not unusual that there is concern about market dominance. If a product is introduced in small or secondary markets and is methodically evaluated and well received, there is always the possibility that a larger, well-capitalized competitor could bring a similar product into larger markets first. This makes the original product look as if *it* is the imitator and second best. So the major fast break is a preemptive strike, getting to market first and staking a claim.

This introduces another reason to consider the fast alternative: what to do when you're *not* first.

Your product may be in development or even still in the idea stage when a competitor launches a similar or almost identical product. Coincidence? Conspiracy? Industrial espionage? For purposes of this example, the reason doesn't matter. All that matters is that whether or not your product is better, someone else is out there first, getting consumers to test the product and tell about it. Moments like this give birth to colorful slogans such as "You have tried the rest, now try the best." If you are forced to play catch-up, the slower approach won't do. The faster approach will probably need to be expanded and enhanced to include add-ons such as celebrity spokespersons and endorsements, discount coupons, and perhaps even a contest or sweepstakes. It's full speed ahead, not just to catch up, but to *overtake* the other brand.

An example of this situation is the Great Wine Cooler Wars of the 1980s. Well, perhaps not *wars*, but certainly some spirited competition. Wine coolers were basically a reintroduction of the "pop wines" of the '60s and '70s. The first major advertising in the category, for California Coolers, was an instant hit. Gallo wineries came second with their Bartles & Jaymes brand. A clever and hugely popular TV ad campaign, supported by high-profile print and in-store displays and a substantial ad budget, was critical to Gallo's brand rapidly becoming the category leader.

Alas, by the time Seagram's, another giant in the spirits industry, entered the cooler business, even the company's Hollywood movie stars and their seven-figure endorsement deals couldn't catch up to Bartles & Jaymes fast enough to be a threat. The brand remained number one until the category pretty much "fizzled" in 1990, a product whose time had come and gone. Again.

A number of companies have chosen to act as sole sponsor of non-media events. Some of the advantages of such an approach are increased name recognition and the opportunity to promote a very positive image. These events make the sponsor appear to be not only interested in selling a product, but also dedicated to promoting an event that will benefit the community—with some strings attached. Examples of companies using non-media event sponsorships to help build star-quality brands are

Volvo Tennis
The Kemper Open
The Firestone 500
The Bud (Budweiser)
  Triathlon

The Virginia Slims Open
Tour d'Trump
The Marlboro Grand Prix

Positioning Your Brand

A popular, overused, and sometimes confusing term in marketing is *positioning*. Al Ries and Jack Trout used it as the title of their 1986 book and described it as "a new approach to communication." They took the stance that positioning is not something a company does with a product, but something that takes place in the mind of the prospective buyer of that product.

Professor David Aaker believes, "Positioning is closely related to the association and image concepts, except that it implies a frame of reference, the reference point usually being competition."

When marketers speak of positioning a product, they mean all of that and more. To position a product can mean to attempt to conjure an image or an association in a mental frame of reference, to physically place it in a particular section of the store, or to make it available through a related service where one may expect to find it.

For example, personal items or clothing sold in a shop located within a fine hotel may be logical merchandise for the traveler who suddenly finds himself or herself in need of something inadvertently left at home or unexpectedly needed. However, an upscale hotel would by intention not carry a low-priced or even a medium-priced item or line of clothing not in keeping with the hotel's own image, much less that of the guest who would choose to stay there.

Thus, a particular brand of clothing would be *positioned* as being of a certain predictably high level of quality. The guest would expect it. Of course, the guest also assumes that higher prices reflect both the convenience of having the item available as well as its higher quality. This logic extends to purchases of simple items, such as a nail file or a package of chewing gum, which may be priced at double or triple (or more) the normal price because of their *position* within an upscale establishment.

Vitamins or other nutritional supplements "sold only through health food stores or fitness centers" distinguish— or position—themselves against brands that are mass marketed (usually at a much lower price) in drugstores, supermarkets, or discount chain stores. The location of the business itself and the physical placement of the product within that environment make a strong statement to customers as to how they are to regard the product relative to its more commonly available competition.

The product whose advertising or label carries the words "sold only in fine specialty stores" is hoping to infer a level of particularly high or unique quality without ever actually having to make that claim. The suggestion is that the product must indeed be special to be sold only in these unique, special places. This is how the product has been *positioned* in the customer's mind.

This is, in point of fact, very effective marketing.

A classic positioning story is Wheaties—the breakfast of champions! This popular breakfast cereal would often feature a picture of a superstar athlete on its box. If this cereal is good enough for the great legends of most every sport, it should be right for a growing kid. That's not just celebrity endorsement, it's positioning. And the manufacturer, General Mills, seemed happy enough to ignore the fantasies of children who hoped to grow up to be teachers, physicists, or real estate developers. Wheaties boxes spoke to the football, baseball, basketball, soccer, hockey, swimming, or tennis stars of tomorrow—which, the company was assuming, pretty much took in most kids.

The simplicity of Apple Computer ads, emphasizing terms like "user friendly," told the nervous, nontechnical types not only that there was nothing to *fear*, but that this thing was actually *friendly*.

Positioning a product is, of course, not the same as advertising it. "Breakfast of Champions," for example, appeared in ads for the product, but it also appeared on the packaging, on premiums, and in various promotions. It was a positioning statement that sought to help differentiate the brand among other popular breakfast cereals in its category, Kellogg's Corn flakes, Cheerios, and Post Raisin Bran.

Advertising is perhaps the most inclusively effective component of the marketing plan. Promotions, publicity, sponsorships, and special events all contribute to help-ing to differentiate the product from competitors, but advertising typically reaches the most people in the most controlled sales-inducing environment. This is a major consideration in attempting to successfully position your brand.

Developing Your Marketing Plan

No product, regardless of how large or small the company, should be brought to market without a carefully defined marketing plan. Your marketing plan, while touching many of the same bases as your competitors, should be designed to emphasize your uniqueness. Like the corporate identity manual, marketing plans may be a single-page checklist or a thick volume. Like most other manuals, the thicker they are the less likely they are to be used.

Your marketing plan is your basic road map, setting out the tone, pace, direction, parameters, and costs of getting you where you want to go. It should be realistic in terms of goals and budgets. Typically, a marketing plan follows an outline that includes the following:

I. **Situation Analysis**

A. Your own position

B. Your competition

C. Government and regulatory considerations

D. Public attitudes toward your product, your company, and your competition—both alone and relative to you and/or other competitors

II. **Objectives**

A. Your overall goal in terms of sales, market share, changes in attitudes and awareness

B. Timetable for achieving your objectives

III. Strategy

To some, a marketing plan represents a strategy in and of itself. Your strategy should define how you expect to achieve your objectives.

IV. Tactics

The approach to implementing your strategy, such as advertising, publicity, public relations, special events, lobbying regulators or legislators, and/or promotions

V. Evaluation

A. Establishing benchmarks for achieving objections

B. Revision of strategy and tactics, if needed

Above and below each of these points is the issue of budget. The goals of your marketing plan should be realistic in terms of not only their ability to be met creatively, but your ability to fund your strategy and the tactics to achieve it. To that end, your marketing plan also requires flexibility.

University of Tulsa marketing professor Robert D. Hisrich notes, "In order to carry out effective planning and control, managers must have relevant and accurate information on a continual basis." The relevant and accurate information to which the professor is referring is *research*, an essential component of every marketing plan and, hopefully, a part of every budget.

Again, it doesn't matter how large or small the company or the goals of the brand; going into the marketplace without a marketing plan and current market research is like flying without radar. You might reach your destination, but do you really want to maximize your risks?

Some companies spend enormous amounts of money on research, such as multipage questionnaires, phone surveys, focus groups, and demographic or psychographic studies. Others rely on more modestly acquired data from customers, dealers, and sales reps. Somewhere in between these two extremes is likely to be an adequate picture of your market. Most major business and trade publications have considerable market research data on file, which they are usually delighted to make available to their advertisers.

A typical issue of *American Demographics* magazine offers information on trends and buying habits that once cost individual companies thousands of dollars to compile. Research firms have newsletters and studies available on almost any subject; the advent of the Internet has made access to volumes of information on a global level simple and highly cost-efficient.

However one acquires it, reliable research can mean the difference between hitting a target dead-on and making very costly mistakes. A CEO or a manager who dismisses or minimizes the need for research, claiming to know his or her market, product, or prospect certainly might be right. But doing business under the best of circumstances carries enough risks and variables. Why add to them?

Before rolling out a new brand, determine:

1. What is the potential market for this product or service?
2. Who is your customer?
   a. male, female, or both; child, parent, families, single parents, students, senior citizens, and so on
   b. income
   c. geographic area or region
   d. education
   e. lifestyle or ethnicity, if relevant
3. Who/What is your competition?
   a. company
   b. product or service
   c. size relative to your own
   d. budget relative to your own
   e. history, alone and relative to your own

4. How are you (company *and* product) perceived by your market, alone and relative to your competition?

5. Has anyone tried to achieve your objectives with the same type of product or service and failed?

6. How important a consideration is the reputation of your product or company in the minds of your customers?

7. Does this product complement or compete with another product of your company?

Adding Value to a Brand

Exactly what constitutes value is subject to change.

Some companies painstakingly build up their brands over the years. They use huge advertising and marketing budgets, some physically positioning themselves conveniently (at the corner store, in your community, etc.), some through referrals and word-of-mouth advertising, and some through the quality of their service or their guarantee.

At least two generations made Sears "where America shops" partly because of the store's practically lifetime guarantee. Customers could buy something at a Sears store in Chicago and, if not completely satisfied, return it to a Sears store in Miami or Detroit or wherever was most convenient for the customer. The Sears name meant service and value, and the company's stores were located in the most heavily populated areas. As if that weren't convenient enough, purchases and returns could be handled by mail or Sears's own personal delivery service.

Ironically, Sears lost its preeminence as the world's largest retailer to Kmart and Wal-Mart, two operations with stores *not* in heavily populated areas, but on the outskirts of major cities. Both Sears rivals put price ahead of service and found customers were willing to travel farther, wait in longer checkout lines, and accept only a manufacturer's guarantee (if one were offered) over the stores' own promise of satisfaction.

Value clearly did not mean the same thing to everyone. This point underscores the importance of ongoing market research to track trends and shifts in public tastes and preferences, as well as changes in priorities. To a certain segment of the market, the higher price tag of a Cadillac, Lincoln, or BMW will always represent a certain standard of quality and value. They can afford it. But in less economically prosperous times or when greater cost-consciousness is evident, quality and value may need to be redefined. The marketer operating under such conditions must:

1. Reconsider or redefine the target market
2. Reposition the product
3. Change the product
4. Perhaps do all of the above

In some cases, cutting prices can produce the opposite effect of the one desired. When BMW announced that it would be introducing a lower-priced model for the belt-tightening of the 1990s, reaction was very negative from BMW owners who saw the status and potential value of their brand being diminished.

When Cadillac took note of the trend in public tastes for smaller, more fuel-efficient cars, they sought to move away from the brand's image as a large "gas guzzler" by introducing a smaller model. It flopped. Cadillac buyers wanted not only luxury and status, but also the *image* of luxury and status; they didn't want just another choice in the crowded field of compact cars.

How might these two auto giants, both with a history of understanding the psychographic makeup of their customer base, have responded differently?

One way would have been to simply *ask their current customers* how they felt about altering the image of these prized and pricey products, rather than considering only the possible preferences of potential customers. The companies might have shown a certain highly exploitable respect for the people who make up their market by introducing a new line with phrases such as "you asked for it" or "our customers told us what they wanted most in a luxury car." Enhancing the value of a service package by providing a stronger warranty or a trade-in or upgrade option adds value without diminishing the perception of quality or desirability. When Volvo cited the number of years that its cars were on the road (more than most people probably assumed), the message of the ad was that a Volvo was worth the extra money it cost. Showing the cost savings in replacement parts, as compared with those of a lesser product, is another way of saying lower price alone doesn't mean value.

Research not only must tell you which trends might be influencing your customers, but should help you keep your finger on their pulse. Do they define the terms *quality, convenience, service,* and *value* as they did when you last conducted market research? Tastes change. Monitoring customer satisfaction is as important to the success of your brand as initially defining your target prospect.

Airline mileage points, bonus points programs from American Express or Marriott Hotels, cash rebates from Discover Card, merchandise checks from GE Rewards Visa card, extra time to pay on a revolving charge, and lower financing rates have all replaced the value-added concept that was pioneered by Blue Chip, Plaid, Top Value, Gold Bell, and S&H Green Stamps a generation ago. It is not surprising to marketers that even the most upscale customers appreciate getting more for their money. Companies and products that do well over time, maintaining a loyal customer base, are the ones that strive to give more—or at least the *perception* of more—to their customers.

This is not to suggest a practice of deceiving customers. Remember that much of what has been outlined in this section (the use of images, associations, and points of differentiation) represents both practical distinctions and emotional distinctions. Making customers *feel good* about a product qualifies as added value. Perhaps they feel good because they've saved money on the giant economy size, or because the product is good for the environment, or because a percentage of the manufacturer's profits benefit the Special Olympics.

People will often choose a brand for intangible reasons, especially if the right message guides them to do so. There is nothing deceptive in finding and exploiting value in the brand or in how it is marketed.

About Brand Distribution

It might seem as though a discussion of distribution should be about *product* distribution and, of course, it is. But consider how certain lines—Amway, Avon, Mary Kay, NuSkin, and Tupperware, to name only a few—distribute their products exclusively through direct home sales, typically via multilevel marketing groups.

Part of the special appeal of many of these products is that this is the *only* way they may be acquired. In that respect, brand distribution becomes a part of brand building. Other names, such as Ronco, K-tel, and Candlelight Music, built their reputations by selling a myriad of products through "exclusive TV offers." True, this is advertising, not distribution per se, but the brand focus is on suggesting limited accessibility and exclusivity.

A phenomenon of the 1980s was the "infomercial"—a program-length television commercial—in which a wide variety of products and services were offered within the context of simulated news shows, talk shows, entertainment programs, and game shows. The range of products around which these programs were built included treasuries of recorded music, hair care products and makeup makeovers, diet programs, real estate courses, and a seemingly unlimited number of self-help programs, available "for a limited time only... and only from this 800-number."

The Body Shop offered its own lines of quality personal care products exclusively at its own worldwide chain of stores. Customers were encouraged to travel the possible extra distance and pay a possibly higher price than for competitors' brands in order to patronize stores that were pro-environment and anti-animal-testing, and that donated portions of their proceeds to these causes. Literature on these issues was distributed throughout the stores. Having a Body Shop brand product in your home not only suggested your willingness to "go the extra mile" to find the shop and pay the price, but also stood as a political statement about your position on ecology and animal rights. Many customers find a certain cachet in that.

Other enterprises, such as Lands' End, L. L. Bean, and Victoria's Secret, offer their branded merchandise in a limited number of stores bearing their respective names, but they mainly sell to catalog shoppers who never leave home, preferring to shop by mail, phone, or the Internet, an enormously thriving and growing market segment.

Under normal circumstances, distribution is a major factor in brand marketing. That is, if a product can be sold through a major upscale chain store, its very presence represents a certain assumed or perceived level of integrity, acceptance, and quality. Additionally, the *volume* of product sold is large because the chain itself is large. The exposure on such a large scale makes a difference.

The expression "under normal circumstances" is important to note, because what is normal changes with market conditions. Products such as the Juice King, the Thighmaster, the Veg-o-Matic, or the Deal-a-Meal weight-loss program would have had to spend months with large colorful displays blocking the aisles of Wal-Mart, Kmart, or your local supermarket before any hope of profit might have been realized. But a series of 60-second TV spots, scattered across the country during the cheapest times of day on secondary TV and cable stations, sold millions of units of the products, often without even inventories being maintained.

Another brand distribution relationship involves telemarketing, an area that constantly draws public wrath, sometimes even more than television commercials. Complaints constantly pour into regulatory agencies, consumer advocate organizations, and the media about the frequent, intrusive phone calls that interrupt sleep, meals, and life itself. Yet enormous sales result from telemarketing—from magazine subscriptions and credit card insurance to season theater tickets and time-share condos. While the process of telemarketing is a *sales* process, the product being marketed has a form of brand distribution exclusivity.

Despite the criticism of multilevel marketing operations as "pyramid schemes," there are few methods of marketing as effective at generating interest, awareness, and sales as the word-of-mouth presentation and endorsement from a friend or neighbor who asks for the order as well as for the names of other people to call.

Unrequested postal deliveries introducing new products or brands or offering "special low prices for buying direct" were usually addressed to "Occupant" at your address. This was called junk mail. Soon, however, such mailings evolved into carefully and scientifically developed lists, based on demographic and psychographic data. These mailings were the foundation of what came to be called *direct marketing*, which for several years was the darling of the advertising and marketing industry as a targeted alternative to the traditional media buy.

Typical avenues of distribution have included retail specialty and department stores, discount stores, supermarkets, superstores, and, depending on the product, mail-order catalogs, door-to-door sales, and even vending machines.

With modern computer technology, the Internet, and satellite and cable television, the avenues have widened. Mail and phone lists are more finely targeted, accurate, and personalized. TV is more finely tuned with sports channels, science fiction channels, news channels, and a variety of "home shopping networks" which, despite a professed hatred of commercials, audiences tune into hour after hour, watching sales pitches and calling the toll-free numbers to amass their purchases.

Distribution is as much a function of marketing as it is a function of operations. Think of brand distribution as part of the brand-building process. Understand that *how* a product is distributed is often a factor in how people relate to it—as either unique and special or as part of a pile of other products. If advertising is supposed to utilize a unique selling proposition (USP) or distinguish one brand from another, a creative approach to distribution could be a part of that proposition or even the proposition itself.

Building Your Brand

1. Price and quality equal value. Value—or the *perception* of value—is why people choose one brand over another. Identify the value in your product or service.

2. Image, reputation, status, or that "feel good" quality, is an important component in value.

3. There is a measurable relationship between a brand's level of public awareness and its market share.

4. Create a marketing plan and continually adjust and fine-tune
it into a road map for a brand-marketing success.

5. Position your brand in the right place physically and geographically, as well as in the mind of the

consumer, both alone and relative to your competition.

6. Clearly differentiate your brand from that of your competition. find its unique selling proposition (USP).

7. Consider creative methods of distribution as a part of your brand-building process.

3

Building Brand Loyalty

"The loyalties which centre upon number one are enormous."
> —*Winston Churchill (in 1949)*

"You're in good hands with Allstate."
> —*Allstate Insurance Company*

A s each generation comes of age, the term *nostalgia* takes on its own meaning for them. As years go by, marketers become more adept at defining the target market and calling upon affectionate remembrances of things past to serve as advertising points of reference . . . and using them to sell product. The old magazines piled up for years in the garage are now selling for 20 times their cover prices at the old nostalgia shop. Tapping old memories can be very profitable.

Whatever Became of Brand X?

A prime example of this retro-advertising involves one of the most affectionate campaigns in the late 1980s, for the antacid Alka-Seltzer. It involved a reframing of a black-and-white commercial for the product from some 30 years earlier. Baby boomers sat smiling, watching the animated character "Speedy" come out of retirement, looking none the worse for wear and cheerfully selling a lot of antacid.

The Nestlé Company brought back a nearly 40-year-old idea, a television spot using *Farfel*, the sleepy-eyed puppet dog of ventriloquist Jimmy Nelson. Nelson still did the voices, but he did them off-screen, no longer appearing in the ads. While the puppet looked the same as the now-adult viewers remembered, the youthful puppeteer, of course, did not.

7-Up resumed calling itself the "Uncola." After a lengthy absence, despite changing its signature from Kentucky Fried Chicken to the less cholesterol-intensive sounding KFC, the KFC brand managers remembered to tell the audience "We do chicken right," a very popular theme line for the product from many years earlier.

While some brands continue to do well and are, indeed, a virtual part of the landscape, bringing a flash of instant recognition and appreciation, others have become part of the history of brand marketing and answers to trivia questions. The March 11, 1957, issue of *Life* magazine featured on its cover a young U.S. Senator John F. Kennedy. The issue, an accurate mirror of the time, carried some 125 ads. Among the advertised brands that could still be recognized effortlessly nearly 50 years later were

Allstate Insurance	Hunt's Tomato Sauce
American Dairy Association	Imperial Margarine
Arrow Shirts	John Hancock Insurance
Bayer Aspirin	Kellogg's Rice Krispies
Betty Crocker cake mix	Lipton Tea
Birdseye frozen vegetables	Maytag
Campbell's soup	Mercury
Canadian Club	Pepsi-Cola
Chevrolet	Pontiac
Colgate toothpaste	Ritz crackers

Drano
Ford
Fruit of the Loom
General Electric

Scripto pens
7-Up
Smirnoff vodka
Texaco

Other ads appearing in the same magazine were for brands that may not seem quite so familiar. The products or companies, once popular, have either ceased to exist or have so diminished in market presence that they might as well have ceased to exist. When did anyone last see these largely bygone brands?

Bestform girdles and bras
Bluettes and Ebonettes rubber gloves
Duplicolor auto touch-up paint
Evening in Paris deodorant
L&M Cigarettes
Musterole pain ointment
River brand rice
Schrank's Dreamwear
Snow Crop (frozen fruits and vegetables)
Stanback headache powders and tablets
Style-Mart Gulftone clothes
Tempo— "the quick mix for meatloaf!"
Tru-Glo Liquid Make-up
Veto deodorants

Please note that the following major national brands of soap, cars, and cigarettes (a *lot* of cigarettes) went out without a bang. They just quietly fell from prominence to become footnotes in the history of brand names:

Acnecare
American Family flakes
American Family Snow
Bel-Air cigarettes

Ipana Toothpaste
Kaiser-Frazer motor cars
Mum deodorant
Nash motor cars

Burgess batteries

Candettes lozenges

Chum Gum

Clapp's baby food

DeSoto motor cars

Dr. Lyon's Tooth Powder

Duz detergent

Edsel motor cars

Herbert Tareyton cigarettes

Hudson motor cars

Old Gold cigarette

Old Nick candy bars

Packard motor cars

Paxton cigarettes

Philip Morris cigarettes

Raleigh cigarettes

Rinso detergent

Spring cigarettes

Tip Top bread

York cigarettes

Most people can recall a long-gone brand from childhood and ask "Whatever became of . . . ?" Was it a lack of advertising or marketing support? Changing tastes or trends? A flawed marketing strategy? Perhaps simply a bad product that deserved to die a slow and unnoticed death?

Could the company have been driven out of business by an unscrupulous multinational conglomerate? Maybe.

Maybe it was one or all of these reasons, but very likely ongoing market research—taking the pulse of the market—and a plan that anticipated worst-case scenarios could have kept some of these names a part of contemporary life.

A marketing plan will define, position, and lay out a strategy to build a brand. Very often after achieving acceptance and healthy sales, a brand will become a *name brand*, established and successful, hanging back while new, aggressively marketed brands knock it not simply off the top, but into oblivion. If that sounds like an overstatement, look again at the list of bygone names. True, there a lot of now-defunct cigarette brands on the list. One could make the point that, with cigarette smoking so heavily under attack, that was inevitable. But was it? Brands such as Marlboro, Winston, Camel, and Kool were around at the same time as the others, and despite the shift in public sentiment regarding smoking, they continued to prosper. Were they simply better products? The likelihood is that they were better-cared-for brands.

To the matter of survival of the fittest (defined as strong and well capitalized), it is again a function of a good marketing plan. The plan must provide for building not only brand *awareness* but also brand *loyalty*.

About Brand Loyalty

In test markets, beverage manufacturers know that if people don't like the taste of a product, they won't buy it. Not even *once*. But marketers know they cannot assume that just because consumers *like* a product and even buy it a few times they will become regular, loyal customers.

Brand loyalty never just happens. Brand managers have to make it happen.

There are the exceptions, of course. Sometimes brand loyalty does occur through no effort of the marketer. Sometimes, even when a product is not promoted, it presents an attractive image to a particular consumer segment.

A would-be novelist admitted that he greatly admired the work of Kurt Vonnegut, who writes frequently about the fact that he is a heavy smoker of Pall Mall cigarettes. Based upon that, the would-be novelist became a loyal consumer of the brand himself.

Marketers of Pall Mall might have sought, in the product's best days (at one time the bestselling cigarette brand in the United States), to position the brand to get the attention of the aspiring writer and others. But it is unlikely that they would have suggested any direct connection between the success of Vonnegut as a novelist and his choice of cigarette brand. As an advertising device, use of celebrity endorsers has proved successful. In this instance, it would have been a case of preaching to the choir.

A more mainstream example: some owners of certain cars will proudly announce that they represent second- or third-generation owners of a particular car. It doesn't matter how much or how little the cars are promoted as far as these folks are concerned, they will stick with the brand of choice.

Usually, it isn't that easy.

The brand of choice is a decision usually based on the brand's image and value (price and quality, or the perception of quality). The decision to remain loyal to the brand over time is based on these considerations:

- value (price and quality)
- image (both the brand's own "personality" and its reputation)
- convenience and availability
- satisfaction
- service
- guarantee or warranty

In terms of *value,* long-term use of the brand in one sense suggests loyalty, but much of the responsibility for keeping this going lies with the manufacturer's brand manager. Brand loyalty is not totally customer-driven, nor does it occur in a vacuum.

A lessening of quality standards will disappoint even the most loyal supporters, as will a price change that appears unwarranted. In some cases, it is helpful to advertise the manufacturer's suggested retail price. In the automobile example, where a dealer will typically sell cars for less than the manufacturer's suggested price, everyone looks good. But in the case of a candy bar—where the suggested price is 50 cents but big chain stores sell it for 40 cents—neighborhood, airport, or office-building convenience stores want 95 cents for it, leaving customers to stand in dismay and mumble, "How can they charge that much for *this*?"

At times like that, marketers should advertise the price and leave it to the retailer to explain the concept of overhead to the customer. Too often marketers and manufacturers take the criticism for inflated prices when they are not involved in setting the final item price.

Remember, too, the advantage in publicizing how long it has been since your product has gone without a price increase, while so much else has gone up (perhaps including the price of your competitors' brands). Since even the most affluent consumers enjoy realizing a savings, being able to hold the line on prices increases your ability to claim greater value. Such courtesies to customers go a long way in building brand loyalty.

In some cases, the reverse of this is true. The collectible miniature stuffed animal Beanie Babies were a sell-out sensation of the late 1990s, with customers eagerly awaiting each new addition to the line. Retailers would inflate the selling price of the item, sometimes four to six times its list price, or impose requirements for purchase, such as that a customer must purchase two older Beanie Babies in order to buy a new one. Customers seethed. What the customers didn't know, however, was that the manufacturer was shipping merchandise with complicated conditions: For example, in order to get a shipment of new product, the retailer had to accept a heavy shipment of older product. This left the retailer to face the angry customer, who would be upset over either not being able to get the product or having to pay an inflated price for it.

In marketing, this is the take-the-money-and-run approach. The manufacturer makes out well, unless one considers the retailer's anger toward the manufacturer and the customer's anger toward the retailer which, ultimately, will grow to include the manufacturer. This approach seems intended to promote, over the long haul, customer *dis*loyalty.

Some brands have dealt with the price/value consideration in inflationary times by keeping the price the same and lowering the volume or weight of the product. Others have increased the size of the package or its weight as a way of seeming to justify price increases.

The *image* of a company or brand reminds us to consider a point noted earlier about awareness. As there is a measurable correlation between awareness and market share, so too will there be a connection between a brand's image and its market share. Products publicized as "environmentally friendly" build strong brand loyalty among a large segment of the marketplace. Johnson & Johnson's swift handling of the Tylenol product-tampering matter reinforced its reputation as a company and a brand you could trust. Mobil Oil Corporation's sponsorship of artistic and cultural endeavors, such as public television's *Masterpiece Theater*, raises its profile as a good corporate citizen, earns goodwill, and builds brand loyalty.

The personality a brand takes on is of great importance, as in the case of Virginia Slims cigarettes, marketed to women with the now classic theme line "You've come a long way, baby." Pepsi's "The Pepsi Generation" and "For those who think young," McDonald's "You deserve a break today," Nike's "Just do it!" and the College Fund's "A mind is a terrible thing to waste" are examples of marketers defining the personality of a subject or brand and building a public identification of oneself with the brand that leads to strong brand loyalty.

The reason some people will drive or walk a considerable distance past one service station or fast-food restaurant to get to another is *brand loyalty*. Certainly price and quality are factors, but in most cases, the overriding reason is the brand is the brand of choice and its image is one the customer has come to identify with.

On Convenience and Availability

Convenience and availability can make a difference in creating brand loyalty. A company may run huge ads, touting great sale prices and special discounts to students, seniors, and pet owners, and spend a fortune on mailing coupons and plastic membership cards, but if the location of the business is not convenient (too far away, not in a safe area, known for inadequate parking, not accessible by public transportation), it is doubtful if certain segments of the public will take advantage of the company's generosity.

In an increasingly stressful and demanding society, the brand or company that gets the business is the one that offers products that can be purchased and picked up conveniently, ordered by phone or E-mail, paid for by credit card, delivered within a reasonable time, and easily returned if necessary.

Electronic Convenience and Availability

This section completely disagrees with most of the previous section—*for a certain segment of the market.* The 1990s may well be remembered as the decade during which a half-century of technology came into millions of people's lives in a small metal box. Just as television changed most aspects of people's business and personal lives, the personal computer changed, *or insisted that it would change*, the way people lived and worked, shopped, saved, invested, were entertained, and paid for everything.

In terms of ease and convenience, almost every business has a website or an E-mail address. The person at home or at work can access banks, investment opportunities, and practically every retail, entertainment, and information entity in the world by computer. Thousands of businesses have websites, although many still don't know why. Ads and catalogs are displayed and make ordering or otherwise communicating as easy as a click of a button.

For a particular company or brand to *stand out* on the Web is one of the major challenges marketers will be facing throughout the twenty-first century. For the segment of the public that utilizes computer technology at home or in business, convenience and availability are reality, and a company or store's actual geographic location is irrelevant.

However, it is critical for marketers to understand that there will *always* be a significant segment of the market that will distrust computers, prefer to make eye contact with a living person when purchasing, selling, or providing information, and will want to see and touch actual material and merchandise.

Those who use and love computers are understandably excited about all the wonderful things computers can do, but they are often misled by the enthusiasm of their fellow cyber-travelers who believe that everyone has and uses computers—or that everyone should. It is extremely unwise to make marketing decisions based on misinformation. Go back to step one, and let research help you define your market and how it works.

The Satisfaction Factor

Satisfaction is often why Ford or Chevy owners remain Ford and Chevy owners and why coffeemakers, watches, auto parts, and water heaters tend to be replaced with the latest version of the product bearing the brand being retired. Satisfaction can be very often defined as the collective embodiment of all the other factors of brand loyalty: value, image, convenience, service, and guarantee.

The Service Issue

Service is one of the most overused words and under-delivered commodities in business. *Time* magazine once ran a cover story with the headline "Why is service so bad?" The same story could have appeared many times several years before or several years after it actually appeared. Most surveys reveal that what a customer wants most from a bank, dry cleaner, lawyer, supermarket, accountant, shoe repair shop, post office, and restaurant is service. Business has known this for a very long time, has promised it in ads and signage, yet seems fully inadequate to the task. The *service window, service desk,* or *customer service* department is an operator or clerk to whom the customer is sent—to be told that nothing can be done or to be referred to someone else—or where a form is filled out (having been created specifically for such situations), never to be seen again.

Reasons for a high level of dissatisfaction can often be traced to overpromising. If you can't service your customers in an efficient, courteous, and timely manner, train your employees to be courteous, respectful, and responsive to customer questions and complaints, or deliver, replace, or repair what was promised, then don't tell customers that you can. Promising a level of service you can't deliver will come back to bite you and will leave a lasting smudge on a brand that might be otherwise worthy.

Just as people will not go back to a restaurant with good food and good prices if they receive bad service, people *will* go back to a restaurant with just mediocre food if the service is excellent and if they believe they have been treated well. Brands that are not significantly better than lower-priced competitive brands often enjoy repeat business and brand loyalty because of good service.

Guarantee or Warranty

While not everyone takes advantage of a guarantee or warranty, the mere fact that it is offered adds the perception of greater value to a product. When someone never needs to utilize a guarantee, the result should be an increase in the level of brand loyalty. Information acquired when a customer fills out a card to mail in and activate a guarantee or warranty becomes valuable data about who your customers are. It also provides an opportunity to extend a special offer of additional products or services to preferred customers.

Brand Loyalty Case Studies: Cigarettes

Cigarette smokers offer a good illustration of the unique devotion that is brand loyalty. Smokers will usually stay with the same brand for years without being able to say why. Some will say simply "taste" or that a particular brand is less harsh. The occasional smoker may offer that all cigarettes "taste" pretty much the same; it's questionable if serious smokers could distinguish one brand from another in a blind taste test. Freshness and degree of moisture can alter qualities of cigarettes from the same package. If price were a truly major consideration, everyone would smoke generic cigarettes. Coupons aren't redeemed anywhere near levels that are commensurate with their availability. The brand's image is the major consideration because it so closely seeks to identify with the smoker's own image of himself or herself—whether real or desired. Consider these examples:

- Benson & Hedges—sophisticated
- Virginia Slims—stylish, feminine
- Marlboro—long symbolized by the Marlboro Man (even when smoked by a woman), rugged individualist, a maverick, later a more broad-based sportsman

- Newport—usually identified with cool beaches, the surf, streams, deep woods
- Carleton—reserved, deliberate, conservative
- Kool—freewheeling, free-spirited, cool

These are only six brands out of hundreds, each of which allocates a considerable annual budget largely to defining its image. They spend millions of additional dollars on brand extensions to broaden that image, an area that will be explored in Chapter 5.

Regardless of the quality or "taste," few men are likely to be seen even *purchasing*, much less smoking, Virginia Slims. Marketers encourage this to be so, just as Lucky Strike years ago was positioned as a brand for longshoremen and construction workers, rather than concert pianists.

When surveyed smokers were asked, "If your regular brand were not available . . . ?" a high percentage of those responding said they would go somewhere else to buy the regular brand rather than accept another brand in its place. A commercial some years ago that tried to encourage this practice showed a Tareyton smoker with a black eye and the line "I'd rather fight than switch." While indications are that smokers are not quite inclined to get physical over brands, they *will* go to another shop to demonstrate their brand loyalty.

A brand's advertising and package design are the major factors reflecting its image—silver and gold foil, raised embossed lettering, a coat of arms. The choice of the name for a brand of cigarettes to reflect a particular image is the definitive illustration of building power in a brand. Consider some names and the images they suggest:

Barclay	Lark
Parliament	Spring
Cambridge	Salem
Benson & Hedges	Newport
Chesterfield	Now

York	Eve
Carleton	Kool
Winston	True
Kent	Malibu

Names in the left column suggest sophistication, power, elitism, an old English influence. Names in the right column convey a lighter, more relaxed, less intense, even frivolous image. As controversial as the subject continues to be, cigarette smoking continues to increase worldwide, particularly among young women. Cigarette smoking appears to be declining in the United States. But even with television advertising not permitted and other forms of advertising curtailed, new brands are introduced constantly, primarily through newspaper ads, outdoor displays, and package designs, and they are finding their image-conscious market.

. . . and Beer

Beer is another product that many people insist has but one taste. Beer is beer. Yet brand loyalty is high and passions for particular brands run high as well. Again, it is the brand *image*, more than price or availability, that helps define a beer's loyal consumers. And unlike cigarettes, where a particular word associated with sophistication or silliness will translate an image, beer lovers embrace brand names that don't seem connected with a *product*, much less the people who identify with it and claim it as their choice. Consider

Budweiser	Heinekin
Old Style	Dos-Equis
Coors	Corona
Strohs	Amstel

Old Milwaukee	Kirin
Schlitz	Beck's

Whether domestic or imported, the choice of beer is as correct in the eye of the beholder as the choice of a favorite sports team or rock band. Loyalty can seem almost fanatical. The choice of beer says more about a consumer's personal perception of images than about the taste of beer. It's the image.

Saying Something Nice

It is widely accepted that word-of-mouth advertising is perhaps the most effective type of advertising (and is not, at the present time, under any restrictions imposed by the Federal Trade Commission); loyal brand users make excellent endorsers. There is a certain unique pride that comes through when the customer, whether commenting about a beer, cigarette, sweater, running shoe, luggage, or steak sauce, expresses the sentiment, "That's *my* brand."

Ultimately, successful brand building involves identifying with the customer's desires and giving what he or she wants as to value (price and quality) plus the characteristics of *image* being sought, aspired to, or accepted.

Building brand loyalty involves *continuing* to serve a customer in a satisfactory way. Again, research is the key. People's tastes change. Know when and how you must change with them to remain their brand of choice, their anchor in the sea of change.

Is this contradictory? Sure.

But consider that the typical consumer will change his or her hairstyle (or color), wardrobe, address, and job every so often, yet will remain loyal over a lifetime to a particular toothpaste or breakfast cereal. Research will help you get a picture of your customer, your audience, and track its receptivity to change. Sometimes brand loyalty slips when a consumer feels that the product's standards of excellence are not being maintained. The consumer feels let down. Sometimes a consumer walks away from a product that is trying to appeal to a newer, younger, wider market segment and that has not afforded enough attention to the "old timers" who helped make the product what it is.

Consider these points:

- Know your customer.
- Know what your customer wants.
- Satisfy your customer.
- *Keep* satisfying your customer.
- Know when to stay the same and when to change.
- Believe your research and use it.

A Marketer's Fantasy: Customers Pay to Advertise Your Product

Premiums encourage brand loyalty. Once caps, T-shirts, sweatshirts, jackets, and coffee mugs were given away free to help promote a brand. Today, consumers of all ages are willing to pay (a lot) to wear their favorite brand's logo, whether it is a radio station, TV show, soft drink, or software. Let your research tell you if, and to what degree, your customers respond to premiums and build your catalog accordingly. Think about including beach towels, canvas bags, backpacks, visors, and plates with your logo ingeniously incorporated.

Betty Crocker, Duncan Hines, and Campbell's soup are three brands that have very successfully used cookbooks as both premiums and revenue-generating items. The advantages of such a perfectly mated premium to product are many. The premium serves to constantly reinforce the presence of the brand in the user's home, often out in full view at all times. Mobil Travel Guides are another example of a premium keeping the brand visible and represented, even if and when the product is not.

Disney, Viacom, Universal Studios, Warner Brothers, and Coca-Cola are only a few of the major corporations that have opened chains of stores and created catalogs filled with merchandise all bearing the logo of the company or one of its featured products.

Most TV networks and even cable channels now have "company stores" with unique, stylish merchandise all the while shamelessly promoting a product. Members of the public treat visits to these stores as a major entertainment event, and every item (pretty much all premium-priced) is a vivid advertisement.

The public loves it. It represents another extension of *image*. The 50-year-old who wears a Mickey Mouse necktie or a Davy Crockett coonskin cap to the office is saying, "If I'm not still a kid, at least I'm good-natured. And, by the way, notice that what I'm wearing is the logo of a large international conglomerate and that I have paid considerable money for the purpose of promoting them."

Levi's, Starbucks, DoveBars, Williams-Sonoma, and Blockbuster Video are only a few of the many companies that have contracted with the special products divisions of major record companies to offer CDs or cassettes of selected music in packaging that carries the brand's own logo and signature. It is a way of keeping the brand's logo in the customer's life after the product is gone, while still helping to attach a certain *imagery* to the brand. And, although some are clearly subsidized by the brand, the recordings are often priced comparably to music CDs without a corporate sponsor logo.

Let your research tell you if your customers use or want coupons for discounts on your (and other related) products. If the answer is yes, offer them. It is a solid cross-sell concept that encourages brand loyalty. Banks and credit card companies don't typically offer coupons, but they can give coupons for discounts or complimentary products or services from neighboring restaurants or movie theaters. Such offers generate goodwill while saying "thank you for being our customer."

Newsletters, magazines, and regular mailings and surveys suggest that a company wants both to give and to receive information, enhance value, and keep its name in front of the public however it can.

Philip Morris, Fidelity Investments, and Benetton are only three companies that regularly publish slick, colorful magazines that keep their customers informed of a multitude of things from straight features to personal stories about the brand, products, or industry.

A company's mailing list is a very profitable commodity to rent to other companies, and it is a great device for a company to *use*. Mail to your customers. Include coupons and survey questions that will help you take the pulse of the market and reaffirm your appreciation. At the same time, create opportunities for cross-selling your own and perhaps other related products.

Credit cards, mileage points, cash-back coupons, and trading stamps are a few of the devices developed over the years to build brand loyalty while enhancing value and making things easier for the consumer. They are projected to work well into the twenty-first century as well as they worked in the 1950s, if they are packaged, presented, and promoted in such a way that they are easy to understand, acquire, and access.

Many companies offer bonus dollars, points, or coupons to a customer referring another customer to the brand's own satisfied legion. Book-of-the-Month Club, Columbia Record Club, and others have offered gifts (of course, bearing their name and logo) if a customer brings the brand to the attention of a new customer. It is word-of-mouth advertising being given a nudge and paying off—with a payoff.

Catalogs and sale flyers are a way to put something new with your name on it into a consumer's home or business. These items are often kept around (or passed around) for months.

Certain catalogs, such as J. Peterman and A Common Reader, combine listings of products with engaging descriptions and photographs, even stories, relating to the items. The evolution of this process is the *magalog*, a combination magazine and catalog, which suggests it has value to those who receive it beyond that of an order form. The magalog format allows the sender to present more detailed information about the brand, further setting it apart from its competitors.

Production and mailing costs continue to rise, and this is an area where many companies feel they can cut costs by cutting back. That is a serious mistake. Mailing to customers is not just an effort to get another order *right now*; it is to reinforce your presence in customers' lives. A letter, a catalog cover, a brochure, or a postcard that is addressed to an American Express credit card *member*, a Literary Guild Book Club *member*, a BMW *driver*, or a magazine *subscriber* reinforces the consumer's relationship with the company or product. Blockbuster Video and West Coast Video don't need to incur the cost of printing and issuing millions of plastic membership cards, when any form of identification and a few dollars will allow a customer to rent the tapes. The companies issue the cards to promote a sense of belonging to a particular group in hopes that the customer will experience a feeling of loyalty and thus choose one rental store, instead of renting tapes from the booth in the drug store, grocery store, dry cleaner, or service station.

Building brand loyalty is taking steps to make today's customer tomorrow's customer as well.

Building Your Brand

1. Elements that encourage brand loyalty are
   a. value (price and quality)
   b. image (personality and reputation)
   c. convenience and availability
   d. satisfaction
   e. service
   f. guarantee or warranty
2. Ongoing research should be used to monitor
   a. changes in levels of customer satisfaction
   b. changing public tastes and attitudes
3. Know your customer and what your customer wants, expects, and is willing to accept.
4. Develop interactive vehicles, such as a website, an E-mail address, newsletters, hot lines, opinion surveys, and publications to give and get customer information.
5. Consider premiums—free, affordable, or positioned as collectible—that will make customers feel personally identified or involved with the brand.
6. Consider programs, such as those offering points, dollars, discounts, or other benefits, that encourage customers to buy or make use of the brand more often.
7. Express appreciation to customers. The bigger a company (or more successful a brand) becomes, the more customers can feel distanced from it. In a competitive environment, a clear message of continuing service and appreciation creates or increases customer loyalty.
8. Catalogs, magalogs, sale publications, credit cards, and membership cards reinforce the brand's presence in the customer's life and create a sense of participation between the brand and the customer.
9. Customers want to be assured of their value. Being responsive to customers' questions, comments, concerns, and complaints promotes such reassurance.

10. Overpromising—saying or suggesting that a product or brand will deliver more than it actually does or can—is not only deceptive, but a sure way to diminish or destroy any goodwill or loyalty the customer might have had or sought to have with the company or brand.

4

When a Brand Gets into Trouble

"An event has happened, upon which it is difficult to speak, and impossible to be silent."
—*Edmund Burke (in 1789)*

"We have reached the moment of truth . . ."
—*Author unknown*

Sears, once the largest and most successful retail department store chain, was charged with defrauding customers at its automotive centers across the United States. As if that wasn't bad enough, Sears was also accused of harassing its own credit card customers in violation of federal laws, only to increase the stain on its image by being the subject of a class-action lawsuit for selling credit accounts to a finance company that then immediately raised customers' rates.

- America Online, the largest Internet service provider, experienced a systems failure in which customers were without service for some 20 hours, a situation that reached crisis proportions for AOL's business customers who depended on the service as their primary means of transacting business.

- Denny's, one of America's most popular family restaurant chains, was hit with a series of racial discrimination claims that were showcased on nightly TV newscasts for months.

- Florida Citrus Growers had, in succession, not one, but *three* of its contracted celebrity spokespersons (singer Anita Bryant, radio personality Rush Limbaugh, and actor Burt Reynolds) become the subject of either controversy or scandal, or both, each time bringing highly unwanted attention to the celebrity's connection to the florida growers.

- And then there's O. J. Simpson as a spokesman for Hertz. . . .

Uh-Oh. What Now?

By any measure, these situations qualify as crises of major proportions. Business must respond to a variety of situations on an ongoing basis in ways that address moral, ethical, and legal concerns, delicately balancing decisions that affect the fate of a brand or company and its future commercial viability.

Earlier, the case of AYDS, the diet-plan candy, was noted. When a brand's name is coincidentally the same as that of a disease, it won't help simply to add "new and improved" to the product's label. But this is not to jokingly dismiss problems over which a company's fate hangs in the balance. Sometimes brands get into trouble, losing market share or losing their market altogether, because they were something of a fad product to begin with. Sometimes products are so upstaged by competing products, occasionally even those produced by their own parent company, that they appear to give up the fight and die on the vine.

Consider the matter of wine coolers, touched on in Chapter 2. As far back as one can remember, there has been some version of a drink combining wine with a carbonated beverage. The champagne cocktail was one, the white wine spritzer another. The 1960s and '70s saw the introduction of Annie Greensprings and Boone's Farm wines. These so-called pop wines, sold in quart bottles, combined fruit juice flavorings with wine and club soda, the perfect accompaniment to folk music and tie-dyed clothing. As fads and trends were replaced by new fads and trends and as the popular brands began to slip, the manufacturers did not reinvent or reposition the product. They treated pop wines as if they were as surprised as everyone else that the drink had done so well in the first place. The product was left to fade quietly into the sunset.

In the 1980s the same beverage concept reemerged as the "wine cooler," this time in smaller, stylish bottles sold in four-packs and six-packs. It became a huge success, creating a multimillion-dollar beverage category. As the 1980s passed on, so did most of the '80s tastes and trends, including the wine cooler. It was as though society was prepared to treat decades as modular units, replacing one with another, style and fads intact.

"Trend shops" began appearing as an alternative to more serious research organizations. For fees of up to a million dollars, firms such as the Brain Reserve, Trend Union, and Promostyle would advise such clients as Campbell Soup Company, Kodak, and Pillsbury on what were, or were likely to be, the next big trends.

Why? What about the basics of marketing? Shouldn't the marketing plan have been revised, a new batch of research commissioned, and a new ad campaign created to at least salvage, if not breathe new life into, the multimillion-dollar wine cooler market?

It did appear that some attempt was made to replace, for example, the Bartles & Jaymes characters in the television ads with a new, more mainstream theme. But it remains curious that marketing in the 1980s allowed for giving up on a product or brand as soon as a new one came on the scene.

When a hot new toothpaste with baking soda was successfully launched, so were several more, with manufacturers paying less attention to the solid, established core brands. The baking soda toothpaste, by the way, was from Arm & Hammer, the company that had been suggesting for more than 40 years that baking soda should be used to clean teeth. Was this simply a matter of good timing? Hardly. It was a matter of *good marketing*.

The proliferation of brands continues at high speed. For many years, manufacturers concentrated on building brands. If a product's sales flagged, the manufacturer's predictable response might have been to add a little something to the product (salt, sugar, bleach, lemon, mint, conditioners, baking soda, or whatever) and a little more color to the packaging and roll out the next shipment with the words "new and improved" emblazoned above the name. A product such as Procter & Gamble's Tide has been given the new-and-improved treatment so many times that one has to wonder if the product now bears any resemblance to its ancestor. But it's still selling. *Big*. Procter & Gamble stayed with the brand, supporting it, improving it, and keeping its visibility high as new high-sudsing, low-sudsing, biodegradable, lemon-freshened challengers came and went.

How does a manufacturer or brand manager know when it is time to reposition a product, retire it, or leave it alone?

The market tells you. Sales tell you. Yet, as competition intensifies, reliable research (*not* trend data) can be your best defense against declines in market share. But beyond research, your marketing plan must include action tactics. Just *having* research is not enough. A marketer must put the acquired information to use.

Professor Richard S. Tedlow of the Harvard Graduate School of Business Administration notes, "We have seen how consumer tastes and needs with regard to particular products have changed. . . . We have seen how individual firms have changed—how they have sometimes fallen prey to forces that have aged them and robbed them of what made them great."

One reason so many brands stumble is they willingly surrender their USP (unique selling proposition), choosing to identify themselves with self-serving and generic descriptions.

When Lipper Analytical Services ranks mutual funds in dozens of categories, most of the funds designated as number one in their respective categories rush an ad into the next day's edition of the *Wall Street Journal,* each one humbly congratulating itself.

So the reader gets to see a dozen or more ads in the same issue of the same newspaper, all headlined "We're number one." Putting down the paper, this person may turn on a television set to see a commercial for the number one Ford dealer in town, then a commercial for the number one Buick dealer. By now, the audience is no more impressed by this than it is by gratuitous claims of "fast, dependable service," unique to no one anymore and contradicted by consumer surveys.

"Marketers have made it easy for consumers to trade down and tune out presumably venerable brand names by siphoning ad dollars to fund trade promotions . . . by providing all too similar ad messages, by losing the edge in product innovation. As brand loyalty crumbles, marketers look for new answers," wrote Julie Liesse in *Advertising Age.*

Herb Maneloveg, of New York–based Maneloveg Media Marketing, added, "The true tragedy is that marketers make all kinds of speeches and offer unending press comment, but they do almost nothing to change the way they communicate to their publics who control the destiny of products being marketed. And they seldom come up with quality improvements in their brands to suit consumer needs."

Perhaps most damaging is Maneloveg's parting shot, "Most advertisers don't seek out answers. They're merely trying to get through their current quarter, forgetting about the brand's future."

There is plenty of blame to go around when sales or market share declines. Often, blame is coupled with panic or desperation when careers or big bucks are at stake. And all too often, rather than administering CPR to a gasping brand, marketers and manufacturers will abandon it for the equivalent of "this year's model."

Dave Murphy of the Betty Crocker division of General Mills noted, "Brand credibility brings a convenience of decision making to consumers' lives." With the huge budgets devoted to building brand credibility, it has been surprising to see companies exhibit such a willingness to pull the plug and treat brands themselves as disposable commodities, choosing to take their chances with new names and faces.

By the 1990s, the number of items on supermarket shelves had soared to more than 16,000. With all the new products being offered, one might think the matter of identifying a brand's uniqueness would have taken on an even greater sense of urgency. Alas, the opposite is true. The prevailing wisdom has been that, as with a prize fight or the Indy 500, there can be only one winner. One brand, emerging as the category leader, is allowed to dominate while others fire their marketing directors and accept their minor roles, awaiting the next product or revolution to reinvigorate their competitive energies.

Occasionally, there is a clever exception to the rule of blind deference to the category leader. The first great example of this was Avis. The car rental company developed its theme and most successful advertising campaign ever around the slogan "We're #2. We try harder."

The public reacted positively, unaccustomed to hearing any company advertise itself as being anything other than number one.

Sometimes, however, this approach can go too far. Some brands attempted to exploit achieving any ranking status at all. Buick, for example, created a series of ads bragging that it was the only American-made car to make an independent testing organization's list of top ten cars receiving the fewest complaints from owners, or some such nonsense.

The brand was number five.

✳Many marketers believed a curious (and possibly a low) point had been reached when a brand would brag about being number five at anything.

The good news is that, with all the brands' many faults, consumers, having gotten over well-publicized flirtations with generics, continue to prefer them.

The bad news for brands is that "private label" products, which had never been taken very seriously in a competitive sense, have found a niche and consumer acceptance.

Richard Furash, of the consulting group of Deloitte & Touche, contends, "The problem with branding . . . is that consumer goods marketers are not investing in their brands . . . [and as consumers look for ways to save money] they're finding the quality of the private label products are better."

Once simply dismissed as "store brands" and regarded as lower-priced, lesser-quality products, private label brands have been positioned and marketed as easily equal in quality and, in some cases, equal in price to advertised name brands. Adding words such as "gold" or "premium" to the private label brand has, in many cases, even suggested that the private label was of *superior* quality.

Dunkin' Donuts sells its own brand of coffee (whole bean or ground) to take home by the pound. It has built up a loyal clientele. Eight O'Clock Coffee, a brand originally produced for the A&P grocery chain, has come into its own and is regarded by many consumers as on a par with some gourmet coffees.

✳Many observers add that a reason brands get into trouble is that they operate in a vacuum, viewing themselves alone or only against a major competitor, not considering the product or position from the consumer's perspective. While major brands are beating their chests and bragging, the value to the consumer of considering consumer perspective is totally overlooked./

For many years, a major complaint, often repeated and widely publicized and accepted, has been about the overwhelming number of advertisements and commercials to which a consumer is subjected on an ongoing basis. Advertisers and their ad agencies speak freely about it, acknowledge it as a concern, and then go on about their business. The result is a seeming indifference to consumers' complaints.

As difficult as clutter is to solve, it really needs to be addressed more seriously. The object of advertising is, after all, to be noticed and remembered. Consider that if a two-minute commercial break carries—between the actual commercials, local and network or cable promos, billboards and station identifications—around a dozen identifiable pitches, messages, and announcements, consumer recall would likely be no more than two or three.

On the print side, in Sunday newspapers and in the most popular magazines, the situation is not much better, except that the "shelf life" of the ad favors choosing print. This is not very good news to the healthiest brand, much less to one in trouble or in need of greater impact. Despite the recognition and professed concern, the reason that clutter continues to grow is, of course, the high cost of doing business, which can only be offset by cramming as much advertising as possible into the allotted spaces.

As fashionable as the practice has become, one should not single out the media for blame. Advertisers themselves take too many shortcuts. *Advertising Age* makes the point that "despite the care that manufacturers expend on packaging, their products are often merchandised in a haphazard fashion."

Notes marketing consultant Christopher Hunt, "There are floor displays all over the place.... It's a style that in general runs contrary to the careful merchandising philosophy...."

Whoever told marketers that cluttered display areas entice customers, much less show the product in its best light?

Shelves are there for a reason, and so are aisles, display cases, and counters. Clutter is a consumer turnoff, whether in the aisles of Macy's or on prime-time Sunday night television.

Create displays that fit the space. They will be noticed more and will show the product better. Of course, economics suggests that you put the most product in the space. But it is highly self-defeating to crowd a display area.

Two solutions to advertisement clutter are

1. Consider clearly segregating advertising from programming and editorial material. In print, insert catalogs in newspapers and mailings, or set up freestanding displays. Catalogs, when well done, get read and passed along for longer than the usual magazine. The framework allows creative people wider parameters as well.

   In broadcasting, a clearly separated, say, eight-minute segment at the end of the program might resemble a mini home-shopping program that offers video or audio versions of "blue light specials"—discounts, contests, or special incentives to attentive shoppers. This process poses a tremendous challenge to ad agencies to create commercials that are entertaining enough to hold an audience, which is what they are supposed to do. Consider how movie audiences willingly sit through 10 minutes of "previews"— ads for coming films—if they are well done and entertaining. Entertain and inform; don't push the audience.

2. Simply be more creative. Much of television and radio's answer to standing out in clutter is to be louder. Advertising that is funny, uses music effectively, is well-written and well-photographed, and gives the consumer a reason to pay attention gets noticed. Noise and a lack of creativity, clarity, or information make people resent advertising and label it as insulting and intrusive.

A decline in interest in the brand is not always simply the result of bad ads poorly placed or of the crowded, clumsy use of retail space. It is all too often the result of a manufacturer or marketer moving away from the factors that determined why people believed in the brand in the first place. While not every situation is the same, a basic outline can be constructed to help rebuild or reposition a sagging brand.

When is it too late?

The market will tell you. Sometimes public tastes change so radically, the situation analysis seems to write itself:

- Fuel efficiency's in; big cars are out.

- Health consciousness–raising experts say it is tough times ahead for foods with high fat, sodium, and cholesterol levels.

- A recessionary economy means a smaller market for big-ticket items.

- An increase in environmental awareness suggests a decrease in interest in products that are polluting or nonrecyclable.

- A major product or company scandal makes starting over a more realistic alternative to "just riding it out."

But if the brand's pattern of decline is for reasons other than the preceding five examples, consider how one might create a basic map for return to stability and growth:

- Analyze how in its early days, the brand broke from the pack or met a need that had gone unnoticed. What's changed?

- Revise your marketing plan if you need to. A good marketing plan isn't chiseled in stone; it is flexible enough to accommodate changes in market climate.

- Don't operate in a vacuum. Let research tell you how people's attitudes may have changed toward your company or your product, alone and relative to the competition. Are you considered environmentally friendly? Overpriced? Old fashioned? Part of a bygone era?

- Keep your visibility high. One of the most common and most absurd decisions many businesses continue to make is to cut advertising, public relations, and promotions budgets when times get tough and sales decline—*when they need it most.*

- Take nothing for granted. Don't assume that because your brand has been around a long time that your target market knows you and all you have to offer. Reevaluate your price/quality/image, and if the story is worth telling, tell it. If it's not worth telling, then your value must be redefined and publicized.

- Remember the USP (the unique selling proposition). It is the reason people should want to buy what you have to sell.

- Some of the best names in business faltered before catching on big. (Jell-O, Kleenex, 7-Up, Timex, and Pepsi are a few, while others, such as Chrysler, came back after being counted out.) A positive attitude, a desire to succeed, a good marketing plan, and a strong financial commitment to support the plan can keep a quality brand alive in rough or changing times.

Building Your Brand

1. Conduct and make use of market research. Track sales trends (your own and your competitors) and market trends and act on specific needs, repositioning the brand if necessary.

2. Don't give up on a product prematurely. Very often the media announces "the next big trend" and the public doesn't bite.

3. Do not assume that as your brand becomes more successful your customers care about your success. Stay focused on providing benefits. Being number one is good news for your bank, but customers always want to know *what's in it for them.* Tell them.

4. Improve what may need to be improved—product, price, distribution, packaging, advertising, public relations. It's easier
the earlier you begin to see the need. Waiting isn't always fatal, but it usually is more expensive.

5. The best way to avoid charges of being just part of the advertising clutter is to be *good.* Make your brand advertising stand out among the other advertising the way you make your product stand out from that of your competition.

6. Be sensitive and responsive to changes in the marketplace and in public tastes and perceptions.

7. Keep your marketing plan flexible and don't "operate in a vacuum."

8. Stay visible. A company or a marketer is not really saving anything if advertising and public relations budgets are cut when the company or product needs visibility and goodwill.

9. Keep your unique selling proposition in front of your customer.

10. React well to change.

⤷ Adding Guarantees to service /product
⤷ Make catclouge

SECTION 2

Creating a Brand Niche

*our USP
liquid fert*

5

Brand "Personality" and Extension Positioning— a Brand Marketing Casebook

"Break the mold and make impossible the repetition of a certain type of creation."
—*Author unknown*

"Nothing can be created out of nothing."
—*Lucretius (c. 94–55 B.C.)*

Think of it this way: If the brand is Miss America, the brand's extension is Miss Congeniality. There may be an inherent competition between the two, but in order to be accepted and to succeed, each has to fill its own role and live up to expectations without blatantly upstaging the other.

Stepping Out

Professor David Aaker describes the practice of managing brand equity as capitalizing on the value of a name, and it certainly is that.

Capitalizing can go in several directions. The purest and simplest way is to work with the core product of the brand, nurturing, publicizing, advertising, and enhancing its position. As it becomes more and better established, more highly regarded as a brand of choice, price increases are more easily accepted by the marketplace.

Distribution and shelf space, store position, or listing order are more easily enhanced. Word-of-mouth references raise its level of familiarity. The establishment of real value in the brand name is an achievement of significant proportions.

Yet what has made brand equity such a hot topic among marketers is not merely its achievement, but its expansion in two major areas. One is *licensing,* or *franchising,* allowing the brand name and trademark to be used by someone else, often in categories and industries far removed from that of the brand. The other area is *line* or *brand extension* in the form of new offshoot products of the original brand.

Licensing, about which volumes could be written, benefits a brand on several levels. Licensing generates tremendous revenue when done successfully. Disney Studios, for example, licenses its name, image, and catalog of characters and titles to hundreds of manufacturers worldwide for reproduction on shirts, shoes, sleepwear, bedding, toys, tapes, records and CDs, books, jewelry, furniture, school supplies, foods, and much more. Disney Stores, carrying the company's own branded merchandise exclusively, are thriving in shopping malls around the world. A catalog of Disney merchandise broadens avenues of availability. Disney's primary business, of course, is making movies, providing programs for television, and operating theme parks and hotels. The revenue gained from these prime ventures is enhanced or surpassed by that generated by putting the name on products in which Disney has little or no manufacturing role or capital investment.

The *New York Times* noted in 1998 that companies saw licensing as a low-risk way to build brand awareness, to generate additional revenue, and, in some cases, to attract the attention of different audiences or increase a company's appeal to specific consumer groups.

McDonald's, Coca-Cola, and Playboy are three of many corporations that have licensed their names and logos to lines of clothing. After some initial interest, curiosity, and fad-cult-collectible treatment, the McDonald's and Coca-Cola fashions faded. Playboy continued for many years, however, to sell its name on some pricey items that carried the Playboy image, as defined in its magazine, into real life.

Licensing can be as diverse and sprawling a process as creating franchises and, in effect, leasing the brand company's technology or systems to others. This type of licensing is increasingly popular as brands seek to expand into other countries. The brand keeps its proprietary name and processes and licenses them to local companies more conversant with the climate of the regulatory and public environment. This can significantly preserve the brand company's own capital as well.

Licensing of a name and trademark affords the brand numerous benefits, including

1. Revenue generation
2. Greater brand name visibility
3. The ability to utilize the advertising and marketing apparatus (and often the budget) of others to extend and enhance the value of the brand

The downside of this, of course, is that if the licensed product fails to do well in the marketplace, the brand's good name—into which much has been invested—could be tarnished or otherwise devalued.

Licensing has evolved as an enormous profit center for the entertainment industry. It was used profitably to a degree when cowboy stars such as Gene Autry, Roy Rogers, or Hopalong Cassidy could be found pictured smiling at fans from lunch boxes, coloring books, toys, bedspreads, and clothing. It may have evolved into an art form when marketers began selling rights to dozens of items tied to such properties as *Batman, Star Wars, Dick Tracy,* and *Superman,* generating millions of dollars more in revenue than the films they helped promote. The effect of this was not lost on corporate America, which now sees merchandise catalogs of logo-imprinted goods, from ashtrays to neckties and more, for not only movie tie-ins, but actual branded products.

Consumers can buy banks, cups, and pens in the shape of Planters' Mr. Peanut or beach toys shaped and colored to look like giant rolls of Life Savers candy, Tootsie Rolls, or Charlie the Star-Kist tuna. Items such as these were giveaways a generation ago, but by the 1980s they were significant revenue generators. Nostalgia memorabilia worth big money included Ovaltine shaker mugs; breakfast cereal bowls featuring Kellogg's Snap, Crackle, and Pop; and mugs or toys bearing the faces of the Campbell's soup kids. Old fashioned soda fountain glasses with the Coca-Cola logo were such a sought-after collectible success that the company created an entire catalog of Coke-branded memorabilia.

The big revenue does not come from waiting patiently for a brand's logo to become a source of nostalgia. It comes from launching a well-considered line of products that derives added appeal from the presence of a certain logo and indentifying a particular market segment that will be receptive to it.

The second major area in which brands are stepping out is line extensions. Here, too, there are subcategories and differing definitions. Once a product has been introduced, some people consider it a line extension if it is later offered in package variations or different sizes, from mini or "personal" to small, medium, and large to family pack and giant economy size. These are not actually extensions because the product within the package remains unchanged. It does create legitimate confusion. The marketing manager for a food brand speaks proudly of having some 270 SKUs (stock keeping units). To the uninitiated, this may appear to be 270 separate products. It is actually about 75 different products, many of which are represented in several different sizes and package variations (in jars, fresh frozen, in vacuum-packed bags, and so on). In terms of how the manufacturer must track each item, they might as well be separate products. Similarly, a retailer concerned about management of shelf space thinks of size and package variations as if each is a product in its own right.

Does one product in five different sizes constitute a line extension? To some people, yes; to others, no.

What about shapes? Most major manufacturers of pasta offer basically the same product in the form of spaghetti, shells, lasagna noodles, and anything from elbows to bow ties to angel hair. So if six or eight shapes are offered, do they qualify as line extensions of a brand? The answer is the same: yes, to some; no, to others.

The definition becomes more focused when it comes to flavors. The old definition would have been that a product (ice cream or soft drinks, for example) offered in orange, cherry, lemon, and grape flavors was simply one product available in four flavors. Add strawberry, and to some, you now have one product in *five* flavors; to someone else, you have five different products. Depending on who owns the company and what kind of inventory control program is on the computer, both can be right.

The ice cream company that advertises "31 flavors" doesn't really think it has launched a brand extension each time it drops one flavor and adds another. Yet the soft drink company that introduces a new diet or caffeine-free version of its beverage definitely considers such an introduction not just an addition, but a major extension of the brand.

John Loden, of the marketing communications firm Vicom/FCB, suggests, "In today's fragmented market no single product can appeal to a wide enough group of consumers to maintain a brand-based franchise. In order to attract and hold sophisticated consumers, a brand must offer a variety of choices within its line."

But Loden also warns of the process of cannibalization, the extended brand product drawing away from the core brand rather than from the competition. This has always represented a dilemma of sorts to marketers in every industry. If you *don't* offer a new product, you risk losing a customer who may believe that your competitor is being more responsive to current needs, tastes, or trends. If you *do* offer the new product, however, you risk taking the customer away from your own core or parent brand. Obviously, the latter choice is the preferable alternative, albeit an expensive one.

Philosophically, many marketers simply regard such occurrences as the nature of an ever-changing (however slightly) marketplace. It is all just a part of being and *staying* in business.

Some marketers suggest stabilizing the core brand at maximum strength before attempting to extend it. But sometimes the market won't wait.

In the 1980s, when the market trend was running to products with labels marked "light," "low fat," "cholesterol-free," "caffeine-free," "all-natural," and "recyclable," many brand equity–building plans were interrupted. They had to be revised to reflect this very significant shift in public preferences. In some cases, a brand will be aggressively and expensively repositioned; sometimes it will become more than just a single brand.

The debate on the wisdom of brand extension runs from those who believe that marketers should define and stick to building in and selling the benefits of a good product and not fall victim to expensive whims of a fickle public, to those who believe that to continuously sell a successful product means no more or less than giving the public what it wants.

New products must be introduced quickly and frequently. To ensure the acceptance of these new products, brand positionings must be expanded by a conscious, systematic process. This is a recommendation for a well-developed marketing plan with a more long-range view than merely considering what the public wants *today*.

Yet, in a highly detailed examination of the subject of brand marketing, *Financial World* writer Alexandra Ourusoff notes that "in a saturated marketplace, new product introductions and brand extensions are not the answer they once were. . . . More than 80 percent of products introduced [in 1991] were brand extensions. Experience suggests that 87 percent of those products are likely to fail."

Some of the best names in business have attempted to transfer the power, recognition, and high approval ratings of their brands to new products with results ranging from unsuccessful to, in some cases, very embarrassing. Dial soap, one of the top-selling brands, introduced a new shampoo that failed to generate much in the way of excitement (and sales); Bayer, among the leading brands of aspirin, after losing huge market share to aspirin-free Tylenol, launched its own aspirin-free product to a collective market yawn.

Who's Who (and Who and Who) at the Local Pharmacy

Not very long ago, six products reigned as the common household pain relievers and cold remedies of choice: Anacin, Bayer Aspirin, Bufferin, Dristan, Excedrin, and Tylenol. Each was introduced and heavily promoted as a stand-alone product, effectively meeting the needs of a generation and that generation's children. Then came the '90s. By the early 1990s, these six products were represented by some 44 products, with even more variations planned. Consider

> *Anacin*
> Maximum Strength Anacin
> Aspirin-Free Anacin

Maximum Strength Aspirin-Free Anacin
Aspirin-Free Anacin PM

Bayer Aspirin
Bayer Children's Aspirin
Bayer Select
Bayer Select Sinus Pain Reliever
Extra Strength Bayer Plus
Maximum Strength Bayer Select

Bufferin
Bufferin AF Nite Time
Bufferin Extra Strength
Bufferin Arthritis Strength
Bufferin Caplets

Dristan
Dristan Nasal Spray
Dristan 12-hour Nasal Spray
Dristan Cold
Dristan Cold Maximum Strength
Dristan Cold and flu
Dristan Allergy
Dristan Sinus

Excedrin
Sinus Excedrin
Aspirin-Free Excedrin
Aspirin-Free Excedrin PM
Aspirin-Free Excedrin IB
Aspirin-Free Excedrin Dual
    (for headaches and upset stomach)

Tylenol
Tylenol Cold
Tylenol Cold No Drowsiness Formula
Extra Strength Tylenol PM

Tylenol Liquid Pain Reliever
Tylenol Sinus
Children's Tylenol
Children's Tylenol Drops
Children's Tylenol Elixir
Children's Tylenol Suspension Liquid
Junior Strength Tylenol
Infant Tylenol Drops
Infant Tylenol Elixir
Infant Tylenol Suspension Liquid

Most, if not all, of these products have been offered in a variety of sizes and various forms, such as tablet, liquid, caplets, and gelcaps (most caplets were phased out following instances of alleged product tampering). Are these choices so plentiful because the public demands such a range, or are the brands trying to outdo one another?

Some evidence points to the latter.

Indeed, the choices of extra strength, maximum strength, IB, AF, and PM serve to confuse those who simply want relief from aches, pain, and colds, not to be judges in the medication olympics.

In addition, retailer shelf space is limited. Retailers are always delighted to sell *more* products, but to simply offer more choices to customers (perhaps more than they need or appreciate) is a compound problem. For a well-stocked store shelf to accommodate a brand extension in all its various sizes and forms, it must be at the expense of another product. Of course, this could be considered another case of survival of the fittest, with weaker brands relegated to back-room shelves, but a good marketer needs to be sensitive to the problems and concerns of both the retailer *and* the consumer. Certainly, a top-selling brand wields a certain amount of clout and its prominent presence is an advantage to consumers. But retailers often resent having to fit in a brand extension that has not earned the right to command valuable shelf space.

Your research should be the definitive guide regarding brand extensions. If research indicates the marketplace wants you to extend your brand, *share that research with retailers and customers.* Telling people why they should care about what you've done, and that your actions are in response to public demand, is another example of good marketing. Four variations of six products, each available in at least three sizes, forces some choices people may not appreciate having to make. The process of creating, developing, producing, distributing, and promoting yet another new product is also a very costly endeavor. Remember old adages, such as "Less is more," and determine whether or not your resources might be better committed to producing fewer variations and focusing more on building and maintaining the brand.

Such an argument might seem to suggest a strong case *against* brand extensions.

Not at all.

It is, however, a good idea to aim at a target by first lining it up in your sight. If the opinions of experts are anything to go by, the enthusiasm over brand extensions is more of an exercise in competitive one-upmanship than it is a response to the voice of the market.

Al Ries and Jack Trout compare the brand name to a rubber band, noting that it will stretch, but not beyond a certain point. Furthermore, the more you stretch a name the weaker it becomes."

Consider how the simple process of ordering a cup of coffee in a restaurant used to be followed by a response like "Thank you." Now the usual response is "Regular or decaf?"

How long might it be before ordering a Coke is followed by a response such as "Is that regular Coke Classic? Diet? Caffeine-free? Cherry? Clear or Diet Clear?"

It could happen.

Campbell's Soups

The brand extension decision is a strategic one, since the extensions build upon the associations of the core brand. The Campbell Soup Company, already dominant in the prepared soup category (with a more than 75 percent market share in the 1990s), launched Manhandler, Homestyle, and Special Request, in addition to the existing lines Chunky, Home Cookin', Golden Classic, Gold Label, Creamy Natural, Soup du Jour, Cookbook Classics, and French Chef.

"Each of these," according to Professor David Aaker, "was costly to establish and added to potential for confusion. Eventually, the cost in dollars and confusion to establish such a variety of names may surpass their value in terms of offering associations."

Indeed.

To go a bit further, there is not only a somewhat dubious value to the parent brand to create extensions such as these, but a store section full of such products seems to be *competing* with the Campbell Soup brand and possibly devaluing the name. Does it make more sense for Campbell Soup to simply continue, as it has for years, adding to its ever-growing variety of flavors and increasing its category dominance?

Clearly, consumers would agree to sample, enjoy, and repurchase the offshoot brand products, but at what expense? If it is at the expense of the original Campbell's soups, it is *brand cannibalization*, not extension.

It is uniquely challenging in such situations to respond to apparent trends. The marketplace is ripe and a whole new generation is ready for premium quality, premium price, and all natural. So a "gold label" premium price or quality extension is introduced. But everyone has been assuring loyal customers for years that the finest ingredients need not cost more. What to do?

One method is the "Remember how much you loved it?" approach, in which the familiar name is represented in fully new surroundings, where it is appreciated by a whole new generation that understands quality and why good things last.

Another method is to pursue a *segmented* market, rather than a *fragmented* market. Instead of diluting the brand itself with a spin-off or sub-brand, let your research guide you through the steps again, only this time apply them to the idea of a specific *segment* of the market, not the whole market. For example, your product may appeal to nearly everyone, but a tier of the baby-boomer demographic segment very much wants to more visibly define a personality for itself, something distinctively different from both the previous generation and the mainstream consumer of its own generation. They want to feel . . . *special.* Consider the basic elements of a marketing plan and how they also apply to brand extensions and spin-offs:

- situation analysis
- objectives
- strategy
- tactics
- budget

This time, however, narrow your sights. Consider the possibility that a brand extension may not be the best direction to go in. If the core brand product is not cutting it with the targeted market segment, consider a product that will cut it—a product with its own name, one that will probably include a word such as "premium" or "choice" or "special" and that will clearly distance itself from its parentage.

Wine producers Ernest and Julio Gallo, proud as they may have been of their highly successful line of moderately priced table wines, knew to keep the name (and ownership of the brand) well out of sight in launching the popular

Bartles & Jaymes wine coolers. The target market for the product would not have responded well to the image that came with the Gallo name. *Gallo* wine coolers most assuredly would have been bypassed in a heartbeat by this segment that wanted something of its own.

Mainstream vs. Niche Marketing

Segmentation, fragmentation, niche—there are more ways today than ever before to remind marketers that sometimes the best strategy is not right for everyone, and that one size needn't always fit all.

The general public, a specific market segment, or a specialty niche may *all* be answers to the question "What's my target market?"

- Johnson's Wax's popular furniture polish, Pledge, was a leading brand in regular or lemon-scented aerosol spray. Environmental concerns prompted the creation of non-aerosol pump-spray bottles.

- Crest toothpaste is for everyone, young and old, regardless of language or income. At least it *can* be. The product in its original formula meets the needs of everyone when it comes to a quality dentifrice. But perhaps some people prefer a gel formula, believing that it represents an improvement over the original paste. Or maybe they want a stand-up pump dispenser, which is a bit more modern than the old traditional tube. Or, possibly, some parents who like the product think that a cut-out in the shape of a star at the end of the tube that dispenses the product would be more appealing and encourage more frequent usage by children.

When you can identify a market segment with unique characteristics, one that does not respond in agreement with the mainstream, you have identified a *niche market*: young people, senior citizens, people with regional or ethnic tastes or different levels of affluence.

If the product is a good one and is doing the job, why create a niche extension and risk diluting or cannibalizing the brand and the budget?

There are a couple of answers. First, maybe (hopefully) you have learned from your research and sales data that the product has a greater appeal in a specific area. Concentrating on that niche area may or may not warrant a brand extension to take advantage of areas of preference, while not becoming vulnerable in other niches. If the entire market for the product is concentrated in that niche, perhaps a repositioning of the brand is in order.

Another answer is that (again, hopefully) you have allowed enough flexibility in your marketing plan to accommodate changes that occur over the life of the product, perhaps creating an opportunity for a brand extension or other change. For example, a terrific shampoo does all that it promises but, alas, can leave white or gray hair with a brassy look. A marketer's response to this is to maintain the integrity and quality of the core brand, not tampering with it, and to introduce a brand extension for this specific group. If research tells you that the group is not sufficiently large to justify such a brand extension, consider adding a warning to the original packaging, noting that you've got a swell product, but it is not suitable for everyone.

A good marketing imagination can always come up with ideas for a myriad of products. Be clear about whether your plan is to have a myriad of products, a single product, or a very limited number of products that people need and want, which you can afford to create and produce and sell at a profit.

A Tale of Two Toothpastes: Colgate and Crest

Colgate toothpaste, the giant international Colgate-Palmolive Company's flagship product, has been a solid success for generations. Crest toothpaste is the best-selling dental care name from the competitive giant Procter & Gamble. These two category heavyweights aimed for no particular niche or segment over the years, but they exercised their considerable muscle with retailers and the public, packing the shelves with brand extensions aimed at protecting their huge market share: fluoride, gels, tartar-control formulas, stars, sparkles, kids' formula, and baking soda, in tubes, pumps, and stand-up dispensers. Colgate's Total was hailed as a revolutionary formula developed to fight gingivitis (and won the American Marketing Association's coveted Edison Award for best new product).

At the very first hint of a serious competitive threat, these two brands rolled out the extra ingredient or "new and improved" extension. This type of market-wide response is normally only achievable if

1. Research data is so current and so accurate that it definitively reflects the pulse of the marketplace

2. The company has the massive resources necessary to produce, package, distribute, and publicize the new product extension and to do it with great speed

This explains why and how the biggest brands remain the biggest brands. It is in no small part the result of the companies' having the physical and financial resources to react quickly and give the public what it wants. Colgate and

Crest have not strayed far afield, limiting their non-tooth-paste extensions to such products as toothbrushes and dental floss. It's what their public expects.

. . . and a Tale of Two More: Ultra Brite and Maclean's

Maclean's toothpaste was neither a successful core product nor a successful extension. It was, however, noteworthy enough in its time to inspire at least several imitators from major companies that feared the brand *might* succeed at their expense, cost them market share, and create a market for niche-reaction products. Maclean's was introduced as an "adult" toothpaste and the first brand of toothpaste in memory to not even hint at having a pleasant taste.

The brand's message was having a "powerful whitening ingredient" but, while it tested well for strength, its medicinal taste kept consumers from coming back for more. The product was reformulated to add a dash of peppermint, but by then the public had already made up its mind and Maclean's toothpaste joined the list of hard-to-find brands. It might have done better by simply lowering its sights, accepting a position as a niche brand, and being content with a smaller market share.

Ultra Brite was a brand whose managers saw the potential in Maclean's promise of an "adult brand with extra-whitening power" and quickly rushed out a similar product with a similarly unpleasant taste. The difference was that Ultra Brite *quickly* reformulated with a dash of peppermint and supported its reintroduction with a huge advertising campaign. It all but abandoned the "whiteness" hook and promised instead that "Ultra Brite gives your mouth sex appeal." The new campaign was a hit. Marketers know only too well that not all campaigns built around themes promising sex appeal sell products, but they do get attention, and that attention gave Ultra Brite the time it needed to develop its niche. Although a product of Colgate-Palmolive, the company wisely chose to launch the brand with its own identity, rather than risk a failure of something called "Colgate Ultra Brite," which, had it totally flopped, could have damaged the brand equity of the hugely successful core product. Colgate had never much concerned itself with suggesting its own product gave one's mouth, or anything else, sex appeal.

Blowing Smoke: Selling Brands of Cigarettes When the Tobacco Industry's on Fire

Some marketers, as a matter of conscience, will not work for tobacco companies or handle a cigarette account. Statistics show that the industry's warning "cigarette smoking is hazardous to your health" may be a gross understatement. This presentation, however, deals with marketing, specifically, the marketing of brands. Morality notwithstanding, like it or not, cigarette smoking represents a multibillion-dollar industry with sales and consumption actually *growing* on a worldwide basis.

Thousands of restaurants and other businesses that had advertised a "smoke-free environment" have reinstituted smoking sections in response to public demand, and cigar smoking has experienced a huge resurgence in popularity and respectability.

For purposes of this presentation, the hundreds of brands of cigarettes afford some excellent examples of brand marketing at its most aggressive and dramatic and of the results of marketing efforts gone awry... or simply gone.

Pall Mall

In 1964 Pall Mall was the bestselling brand of cigarettes in America. The brand held a very impressive market share of more than 14 percent. By 1986, its share of market had dropped to less than 3 percent, despite its aggressive attempt to chase smokers' changing tastes with the introduction of Pall Mall filters, Pall Mall Menthols, Pall Mall Golds, Pall Mall 100s, and Pall Mall Menthol 100s.

One reason for the brand's decline might have been its clumsy shift in the pronunciation of its name in television and radio ads. Despite its spelling, for years the brand had been called "pell-mell," which sounded like the old expression meaning, loosely, "all mixed up." In its later incarnations, coinciding with the brand extensions, it was suddenly being pronounced "pawl-mawl" for a more high-brow British sound. The resulting confusion, for which no research is available, likely contributed to the brand losing focus.

A cigarette brand needs an image, something that links it to the smoker as if the visible package, its logo and colors, tells one something about its owner. Pall Mall had gone from a rich, deep red package with a crest and dignified white lettering, to an assortment of red, gold, green, white, and combinations thereof, whose purchasers no longer even knew quite how to pronounce its name.

When a brand loses its image, its identification with and in the minds of its customers, the brand no longer exists for the customers.

Virginia Slims

If Pall Mall faltered for lack of an identity, Virginia Slims is the opposite extreme, the cigarette category's major niche success. Taking note of the increasing momentum, not to mention *publicity*, surrounding the women's movement, the Philip Morris Company in 1968 introduced Virginia

Slims cigarettes with a massive advertising campaign aimed at independent, liberated women and those who identified with that image. The ad campaign's slogan "You've come a long way, baby" has become a classic phrase of modern advertising (although always forgotten is the far less memorable second line "You've got your own cigarette").

In the 1990s, such a line would never have been used to launch a brand and would have been attacked as being patronizing and hopelessly politically incorrect. Instead, it has survived to anchor the successful brand's advertising for more than three decades.

Philip Morris might have simply repositioned its own badly slipping namesake brand in ads depicting strong women, represented with feminist-influenced ad copy, or it could have turned any one of its many brands into a women's cigarette. Instead, it dramatically rolled out a new brand that, from its first appearance, knew what it wanted to be and told a large part of the marketplace, particularly men (statistically in 1968 the overwhelming majority of cigarette smokers) "this one's *not* for you." It was a very calculated move into niche marketing and paid off very well. Except for the simultaneous introduction of a companion menthol brand, the company has not tampered with the brand, and its market share has held steady.

As noted in an earlier chapter, sometimes someone—management, marketer, agency, whoever—decides that it is time for a change. In this case, the classic line ("You've come a long way, baby") that put the brand on the map was replaced with a line that obviously the brand's "powers that be" believed had a more contemporary ring to it: "Virginia Slims—It's a woman thing."

This move has a flaw. While the original line was reflective of the early days of the women's liberation movement, it transcended its period. The replacement line suggests transient period slang. Cigarette brands require a heavy degree of brand loyalty to survive, and loyalty must be more deeply rooted than fashion. The ad campaign can change, as can the models and photography, but when a slogan becomes synonymous with the brand's positioning statement, it needs to be preserved and protected.

Marlboro

Marlboro cigarettes is an amazing success story both as a leading brand and as a classic example of the effectiveness of modern advertising. It developed a strategy and a positioning statement and did not waver from it for decades. The results speak for themselves.

The European president of Marlboro once said, "We are the number one brand in the world. What we wanted was to promote a particular image of adventure, of course, virility . . ."

He can certainly say they did that. For many years, Marlboro was not only the biggest-selling cigarette in the world, but also the world's largest-selling packaged goods product.

A product of the Philip Morris Company, in the 1990s the Marlboro brand was valued at more than $30 million, according to industry analysts. Of some 400 brands of cigarettes, Marlboro consistently held an almost 21 percent market share—more than double that of its closest rival, Winston.

For years the brand was identified with the Marlboro Man, a nameless, rugged cowboy and outdoorsman, largely depicted in television commercials and on billboards.

Cigarette commercials vanished from U.S. television screens in 1971, but the Marlboro Man did not ride off into the sunset. Since then, the brand has been represented in an expanded schedule of outdoor and four-color print ads and in elaborate direct mail programs. The image of the rugged outdoorsman on horseback, against a backdrop of rolling hills, the Western sky, and stirring theme music, is still vivid in the minds of baby boomers and their parents, though it hasn't been seen in decades. The Marlboro Man remains one of the most successful ad concepts of all time. The brand, still promoted in some 180 countries, maintained an annual ad budget throughout the 1990s in the $120 million range, and that was *without* U.S. TV or radio.

"The Marlboro Man is almost a cliché of the power of marketing," notes journalist Eric Clark, adding that "Marlboro advertising is perhaps the most blatantly escapist of all cigarette advertising. It offers transformation for the harried, rushed, and crowded urban man to the open spaces, freshness, and the elemental toughness and simplicity of Marlboro country."

Expanding its campaign message beyond the man himself, the theme "Come to where the flavor is, come to Marlboro country" was launched. The brand embarked upon an even greater expansion, moving into brand extension and offering smokers at least five ways to buy a pack of Marlboro cigarettes. From the original rugged masculine image wrapped in classic red and white, the brand tried for an upscale touch as the red was replaced by gold packaging for Marlboro 100s, a longer version of the king-size cigarette. A modified gold and white wrapping introduced yet another extension, Marlboro Lights, to great success, as the word "light" became commonly added to many products from beer to yogurt. Marlboro did what Pall Mall had done, only better.

Cigarette brands specifically launched and positioned as "lights" (lower tar and nicotine levels), such as True, Carleton, and Now, did not have many options for brand extension. It hardly made sense for them to introduce a *stronger* version of their brands. But Marlboro had no problems in that area. From its full-flavored original to its longer-length 100s to its Lights, and even menthol versions of each, the brand achieved solid success, market acceptance, and number one status. Everything was perfect.

Well, maybe not *perfect*.

Research was indicating that men, traditionally the majority of smokers, were being bombarded with messages about the health hazards of smoking and were inclined to switch to a lighter brand. Despite the popularity of Marlboro Lights, its gold and white packaging was perceived as feminine—good enough to smoke all right, but what about the rugged Marlboro Man? The brand managers saw years of a carefully honed image coming to a crossroads.

Their answer: Marlboro Medium.

The new brand, in an only slightly modified version of the original red and white pack, and only slightly higher in tar and nicotine levels than Lights, told smokers the Man was back.

The smoking public responded with solid sales figures for the newest brand extension. Industry observers noted that these guys didn't get to be number one, and *stay* number one by such a wide margin, by not having the pulse of the marketplace. They established a strong brand and then built upon it with extensions for every taste within the brand parameters. As each of the versions of the product are available in both soft pack and crush-proof box, there are (at least) 10 ways to buy a pack of Marlboro.

When a smoker wants to feel even better about leaving his or her heart in Marlboro country, all that's needed is a quick check of the catalog of Marlboro brand clothing and related Western gear. Being on the Marlboro mailing list means receiving calendars with rugged and beautifully serene photographs of the West, as well as coupons for big discounts on cigarettes and even rebates for grocery money. That's to buy fixin's for the treats described in the lavishly handsome, photo-illustrated piece titled *Marlboro Chuckwagon Cookin': Twelve Authentic Recipes from Marlboro Country*. Starting with the premise that "A cowboy has an appetite ridin' a horse," the hearty recipes include Cowpoke Beans, Red Chili Biscuits, the Tin Plate Special, and Dried Apple Cake, all images to delight an urban cowboy.

Over time, Marlboro has kept a steady course. The brand's managers and its ad agency have continued to update their photography, for example, even discreetly replacing the original Marlboro Man with a younger, athletic trailblazer type. They stayed with that idea, touched up its gray hairs, kept it fresh, and regarded it as a respectful stage on which newer versions of their product may be rolled out. Ironically, around 1954, Marlboro was one of the newly introduced brands of filter cigarettes positioned as likely to appeal to women smokers. It, too, has come a long way, baby—or *cowboy*, as the case may be.

In the 1990s Marlboro was offering "adventure team miles," basically, a retooling of the old trading stamp idea used successfully some 40 years earlier by cigarette ancestor Raleigh. A catalog of *Marlboro Adventure Team Gear*, looking a lot like a scaled-down version of the L. L. Bean catalog, shows camping gear, clothing, sports watches, and accessories of top quality, all branded with the Marlboro logo and only available by redeeming coupons on packages of Marlboro cigarettes.

The Marlboro Adventure Team is an attempt to stretch the Marlboro Man and Marlboro country across rivers, rapids, and hills, beyond a Western theme per se, while still remaining rugged, bold, and adventurous. It is also a brand promotion designed to appeal to the twentysomething "generation X-ers" and the thirtysomething market and baby boomers, encouraging them to spread out across the land . . . wearing the Marlboro logo.

That is truly effective brand extension.

Camel

No discussion of cigarette marketing and brand positioning could overlook Camel, a brand that seems to have been around forever but projects a consistently contemporary image. An antismoking group claimed to have research that revealed children found the Joe Camel character as recognizable as Mickey Mouse. Their conclusion was, of course, that the brand was leading children to smoke by seducing them with cartoon likenesses.

Huh?

Zealots feel strongly about this issue and insist they have damning evidence to support their claim (tobacco company memos and studies, etc.). Psychologists will long debate whether or not a particular image can be the single motivating force in determining behavior, but one thing is certain: the controversy generated far more attention to the Camel brand than its advertising had been able to do.

In a regular-size soft pack, unfiltered Camel was one of several major male-oriented brands. Its package design ran somewhat counter to what modern image makers would have recommended: a profile of a camel (not historically regarded as one of the more cuddly or lovable of animals) in a desert setting. Deserts are hot and dry, two qualities cigarette manufacturers don't like to suggest are synonymous with their products. And yet, Camel did succeed and remained for decades a top-selling brand, even when it was not spending in the same range as its more heavily advertised competitors.

The brand also lacked a clearly defined comparative position. While Newport and Salem were surrounded by images of cool mountain streams and romantic young models and Benson & Hedges projected a bit of snob appeal, Camel seemed to want to get by just saying it was a quality tobacco product, if that's what the customer wanted.

When smokers showed a preference for king-size filter cigarettes, Camel accommodated them. The brand extension did not overwhelm the industry, but the brand held its own competitively. When the trend went to "lights," Camel Lights were launched very successfully, enjoying solid, steady sales. The Camel Man, a rugged individual who seemed to be a product of the good life, was featured in several ads promoting Camel Lights. The cigarette did much better than the ad campaign, which proved quite forgettable.

In the era of the "lights," Camel joined that segment of the category and turned up the marketing by introducing Camel Ultra-Lights, an even lower tar and nicotine version of the brand than Camel Lights. Around the same time, Camel reintroduced an advertising figure that would make the brand the talk of the industry as well as a lightning rod for antismoking activists: Old Joe.

Old Joe, which came to be called by critics "Joe Camel" (a move that marketers thought was both an asset and a liability), was the centerpiece of a very ambitious, big-budget campaign. It showed a very "cool Joe," a "*hip* Joe," in sunglasses and designer clothes, playing the saxophone in neon-drenched nightclubs, shooting pool, and generally evoking an image of a cartoon international playboy on billboards and point-of-sale displays, in four-color magazine ads and pop-up direct mail pieces . . . and in Camel bucks.

As with brands before it, the concept behind the bucks (coupons) on each Camel pack was to collect and redeem them for merchandise from nightshirts to dartboards to denim shirts and bomber jackets. Colorful premium catalogs were published in regularly updated volumes and distributed by the millions. All merchandise featured the cartoon Joe logo character in various settings and poses.

Multiple-pack promotions included free T-shirts, fleece shorts, windbreaker jackets, and free bonus packs of cigarettes. If the choices so far did not seem as if aggressive enough marketing was being practiced, still another brand extension—Camel Wides—was introduced. This thicker, lighter cigarette had a uniquely different size and appeal to smokers of cigarillos and other small cigars. At this time, most public places still permitted cigarette smoking but prohibited the aromatically stronger cigar and pipe smoke.

Even while the jury was still out on whether or not Camel Wides was a success, the brand launched a frontal assault on top-selling Marlboro Lights by introducing Camel Special Lights. Camel may well have had the largest or, as it might have preferred to be described, the *widest* line extension of any cigarette brand in history.

The *Wall Street Journal*, in describing efforts by the R. J. Reynolds tobacco company to boost sales of its three core brands (Winston, Salem, and Camel), noted, "Camel, the first beneficiary of RJR's marketing plan, has so far demonstrated the most success. . . . The brand also has lured fresh recruits with the introduction of Camel Wides and its Camel Cash program, which bestows items like baseball hats, jean jackets, and beach towels on Camel smokers."

Camel cigarettes had introduced The Camel Collection of men's clothing and The Camel Expeditions travel tours. Some people will argue that selling or giving away designer clothing, trips, or merchandise is a questionable way to sell cigarettes. Some, of course, will argue that the very *idea* of selling cigarettes, much less with the use of a lovable cartoon character, should be revisited for a number of reasons. The subject is one about which many people hold strong, even passionate, opinions and lends itself to controversy and debate, as it has for generations. The fact remains that the tobacco industry is a highly competitive, multibillion-dollar industry in which the surviving brands must continually demonstrate creativity and commitment.

Again, the key components for success are reliable research and a well-defined marketing plan. For Camel to have five product variations competing successfully suggests it knew its market, their tastes, lifestyles, and interests, as well as their sensitivities (*ultra*-lights) and sense of humor (a well-dressed cartoon spokesbeast and wacky catalog merchandise). The fact that the brand was successful in an atmosphere thick with controversy is further testament to good product positioning, brand management, and marketing and, most important, to knowing what the market wants.

Activists' attacks on smokers increased in the 1990s and no less a figure than the president of the United States lashed out at tobacco companies. Camel cigarettes and the Joe Camel character in particular were singled out as shameful examples of companies using cartoon characters to induce children to smoke. The issue of children smoking is one that the tobacco companies' public relations departments should be assigned to address, but advertising should be conceived in such a way that it need not be defended. Certainly, a justification for any ad should be reflected in the brand's marketing plan. The idea that, in the modern age, with what is known about the real and possible risks of smoking, tobacco companies or anyone else is encouraging children to smoke is reprehensible. Smoking is an adult pleasure, as civilized society has always had adult pleasures. Choosing to smoke, whether or not to accept such risks, should be a decision left to individuals—*adult* individuals.

That stated, Joe Camel represents little more than the chosen target of a faction that would have attacked the brand and its entire industry anyway. Cartoon characters have been used in ads as long as there have been ads. Has anyone ever suggested that Metropolitan Life's use of Snoopy and the other Charles Schulz Peanuts characters is a way of trying to seduce children into buying life insurance? Such a ludicrous comparison is totally appropriate.

The success of the Camel campaign is the result of eye-catching graphics, but it is also the result of very intensive media buying and very good ads. It is reasonable to conclude that a young person who makes a decision to smoke will not make a choice of brand based on which brand has a cartoon character in its ads. When the brand, bowing to pressure, dropped Joe Camel from its ads in 1998, no measurable decline in market share was noted. The campaign that replaced Old Joe was a spoof of cigarette advertising in general and of charges leveled against Camel ads in particular. The campaign generated some attention within the ad community, but such "inside" stuff does not serve either short-term or long-term interests of the brand.

In the final analysis, the marketplace decides the value of the product, as it should. If a product is positioned badly or is a bad product, no amount of advertising or promotion will keep it alive for very long, much less make it a success. Between soft packs and hard packs (Camel's version of the crush-proof box), Camel cigarettes have been offered in about a dozen or so variations, including regular, filter, Lights, Light 100s, Ultra-Lights, Wides, Wide Lights, Camel 99's Lights, and Special Lights. With some $800 million in sales in the 1990s, it ranked fifth among cigarette brands but appeared to have the greatest number of brand extensions.

Alas, a *non*-success: Joe Camel, with a very elaborate campaign of buttons, posters, bumper stickers, paper plates, and napkins, was offered as a candidate for president. While history books will not likely note the campaign for posterity, those who witnessed it and collected the logo-emblazoned premiums will remember that Old Joe remained "cool."

Martha Stewart Is Everywhere

In 1998, the American Marketing Association presented its Edison Achievement Award to Martha Stewart. Somehow the word *achievement* seems almost an understatement to describe the path Stewart has taken. She is a combination of Betty Crocker, Miss Manners, Barbara Walters, and Bob Vila. She is an author, a television and radio personality, a CEO, an authority on etiquette and entertaining, the embodiment of a sprawling conglomerate, and a *brand*.

It might be more accurate to say that *she* is the brand, and the catalog of products bearing her name are the extensions. It is not surprising to learn that Martha Stewart is also the subject of at least two parody magazines, a scathing biography, and a spoof on the network comedy show *Saturday Night Live*. Her detractors can say what they will, but it is hard to argue with her record of accomplishments, any one of which would have been impressive.

Since publication of the 1982 book *Entertaining*, which has gone through at least 30 printings, there have been some two dozen additional books on cooking, decorating,

Martha Stewart is the single most visible example of a person who became not just an endorser or successful franchisor, but an actual brand name on items from books on cooking, crafts, and party planning to TV and radio shows, a magazine, and a website to lines of bedding, paints, and other products for the home. There appear to be no limits on extending the brand to all types of lifestyles—or lives.

Photograph of Martha Stewart products by Karin Gottschalk Marconi.

furniture restoration, parties, weddings, and everything to do with the holidays. A magazine, *Martha Stewart Living*, reports a monthly circulation of more than 2.5 million; the column *Ask Martha* is syndicated to more than 200 newspapers; the daily *Martha Stewart Living* TV program, launched in 1997, was the top-rated new syndicated show that year, seen on some 200 television stations; an *Ask Martha* radio feature, introduced at the same time, runs on about 135 stations; her website records several hundred thousand visits per week; and she is a regular contributor to CBS-TV network news programs.

All this would be enough to keep anyone busy as writer-producer-performer, but what caught the attention of the

American Marketing Association and the business world was Stewart's signature line of *Everyday* bed and bath goods at Kmart (annual sales of approximately $700 million) and *Martha Stewart Everyday Colors* paints ($16 million in sales) at Sears stores. It's amazing that two competing national retail chain stores would carry her signature products, since normally a store would demand exclusivity to represent such a franchise.

She is the chairperson and chief executive officer of Martha Stewart Living Omnimedia LLC, based in New York. In 1997 alone the company earned some $25 million on revenues of $120 million.

What has made Martha Stewart this seemingly one-of-a-kind American success story? More important, can anyone else do it?

Each of the enterprises noted represents businesses and industries that are intensely competitive, yet to succeed at one opens the door to another. An author can expand his or her base to become a columnist or TV-radio personality, and vice versa. Actually, it is more common than not for broadcast personalities to write books and writers to test other media.

Calvin Klein, Ralph Lauren, and Tommy Hilfiger are only three designers who evolved into name brands in fashion, extending then into home furnishings and fragrances. Nearly as long as there have been sports, athletes have endorsed products from baseball bats and tennis shoes to razor blades. But this is more than endorsement. Basketball star Michael Jordan attached his name to a line of athletic footwear, a fragrance, and a restaurant. Clearly, more than just another celebrity presenter, in marketing Jordan is a brand.

Despite the fact that suggesting someone is more unique than Michael Jordan is considered blasphemous in most circles, Martha Stewart is unique. She is neither a designer, a chef, nor a serious writer. She certainly doesn't have the usual background or education one finds in

Michael Jordan Cologne at Carson Pirie Scott • Mc Rae's • Younkers

Can Michael Jordan become another Martha Stewart—that is, in the universe of brand names? He's been called the greatest basketball player of all time, and he has also become identified with Nike, McDonald's, and long-distance phone service. But is the name Michael Jordan enough of a brand to sell a new fragrance? Yes. His one-of-a-kind status makes him brand-name material, a characteristic few, if any, other athletes or celebrities can claim. Kids, don't try this at home.

Designed and distributed by Dijan Fragrances, Inc. Copyright © 1998 www.michael-jordan-cologne.com.

persons who create new paints, fashions, or housewares. Yet she is involved in all these things in a very direct and responsible role. Some would ask how she does it; others would ask how she gets away with it. A shameless self-promoter? Perhaps. But she also *delivers,* assuring her customers and followers that a certain level of quality can be assumed in products bearing her name. And, celebrity status or not, the best brands are those that can deliver value, quality, price, and image.

Although Martha Stewart has put her brand on many products, despite appearances, it didn't happen overnight. The first book was published in 1982, the magazine in 1991, the column in 1995, and the TV program in 1997—the same year the bed and bath goods and paints were rolled out.

There was a progression and not an explosion, as happens when a pop star has a great year and floods the marketplace with merchandise bearing his or her likeness with which the star has no apparent connection. Stewart is not merely a celebrity presenter or endorser, as are others whose likenesses appear on department store fashion lines.

Further, there is a logical connection for each of Stewart's ventures. The television program is a TV version of her magazine, which is seemingly a monthly offshoot of one of her books.

The Martha Stewart ventures are *believable* identifications with her. They are logical extensions of a brand that has been accepted and either defined or responded to a desire within the marketplace for such entities.

In terms of imagery, Stewart has retained an identification with her audience. Despite her wealth and success, she gets dirty working in her garden and displays the same occasional awkwardness when working with a recipe or a picture frame that any member of her audience is likely to experience. She has created a "Can you see yourself in this picture?" feeling, by inviting the audience into one of her party-planning books or her TV kitchen.

When she puts her name to a product, the audience accepts immediately that she has actually had some role in at least *using*, if not actually creating, the product, and that's good enough for her legion of fans and followers.

Charlotte Beers, chairman emeritus of Ogilvy & Mather, described Martha Stewart as "a really elegant teacher," adding, "It's true she can make a pie in four minutes. . . . It's maddening."

Stewart claims the reason the public has accepted her as she has moved into various projects and media is, "I try to treat them (consumers) like my friends and colleagues, and it works if they feel involved."

Certainly there are risks in tying a brand and its image so tightly. In this case, it is clear that Stewart not only *represents* the brand, but that she essentially *is* the brand. Without her full participation and role as "front person," there is no Martha Stewart brand.

On the downside, as brand positioning goes, the consumer of the various lines of products must be an admirer of, or at least neutral about, Martha Stewart to be a viable prospect for the towels, paint, magazine, or TV program. A serious *non*-fan would find the entire operation in all of its manifestations a huge turnoff.

Creating and launching any new brand is difficult and challenging. When the brand is tied to a person—or *is* a person—it comes with the advantages of a following and a celebrated image, as well as any negative baggage that person and image carries. In terms of the dollar volume that the Martha Stewart brand has generated in a few short years, it may not be simple, but she certainly makes it seem *possible.*

Microsoft: The Giant Atop the Mountain Comes Under Attack

Was there ever a case where "number one" was not regarded as the one to beat? By whatever means necessary?

None come to mind. The culture of brands allows for the crowd to cheer for the struggling upstart (especially if the upstart's leader resembles a character from the film *Revenge of the Nerds*), hope the upstart wins, cheer the upstart receiving the crown, and then watch eagerly for someone to try to knock the newly enthroned upstart out of the number-one spot.

Microsoft is a great American success story. Its founder, Bill Gates, brought software to market and the market bought it, to a degree that helped redefine the personal computer's role in the lives of tens of millions of people.

The brand achieved preeminence in its market niche in little more than a decade, and then it began widening that niche by giving the public what it wanted at a time when older, larger companies were ignoring the voice of the market. In 1998, Microsoft's market capitalization surpassed $300 billion.

Brand supremacy was won because Microsoft had an efficient, affordable, available, quality product that nearly everyone with a PC wanted to own.

People have been describing the computer industry as "in its infancy" for decades, and of course, it's true. Each new generation of computers demonstrates by its superior capabilities how limited the previous generations of computers were. But infancy or not, each market cycle demands a winner and, in that category, Bill Gates and Microsoft are far enough ahead of the pack to own that designation.

In his 1995 book *The Road Ahead*, Gates wrote, "It seems as though every week some company or consortium announces it has won the race to build the information super highway. Incessant hoopla about megamergers and bold investments has created a gold rush atmosphere—people and companies pressing headlong toward an opportunity, hoping to cross a finish line or stake a claim they believe will assure them of success. . . . But the truth is that in this race everyone is barely at the starting line."

The most popular computer software is often some of the least advertised. The plethora of popular consumer publications is constantly reviewing what's new, what's interesting, what people want, and what techies are talking about. Point-of-sale displays are more effective for software than for many other products. Internet users share much with fellow Internet users regarding what's good. Word-of-mouth advertising, long regarded as the best and most difficult kind of advertising to get, is more a serious force in technology circles than perhaps in any other field.

As a brand, Microsoft had both a sense of what the marketplace wanted and a vision of the products it wanted to present. It became quickly known through trade publication reports and mass merchandising and by its placement as the software of choice, already installed in many top brands of personal computers sold.

The *New York Times* noted, "The company is planning many products, some that are directly involved with Internet access and others that go far afield. In consumer electronics, Microsoft is working hard to reach a simple goal: putting its technology everywhere."

This was the stuff that dreams are made of, but just as dreamers can be jarred awake, the success of Microsoft made it an irresistible target. Microsoft had become the Goliath of the computer software industry. Even the largest telephone company or communications network seemed like a second-string upstart in terms of power and influence, compared with Microsoft. While this (on one level) exalted status brought the company incredible success, it certainly brought more than a little grief.

Being number one meant Microsoft was regarded by competitors as the one to beat. In conducting itself in a manner befitting a market leader, it became the most visible and highly promoted. The introduction of Windows 95 was grandly promoted on a level with a national event or a papal visit. Its theme music was no less than the Rolling Stones performing their hit *Start Me Up*.

Many consumers thought the launch was over the top. It was, after all, only computer software, even if it was Microsoft. Further, reviews of the product were mixed at best, with suggestions that it included vastly more "bells and whistles" than were necessary or desired.

Microsoft could not soften criticism at this stage by appearing small, so its best strategy was to go for "benevolent," the kindly firm that is patriarchal and sets the standard for being service-oriented. Such a strategy works best when it is accompanied by a very visible philanthropic presentation, such as donating computers to a children's center, senior center, or a school and providing the training necessary to put the system to use. Whatever else critics of the company or its products might say, it is difficult to attack public generosity (unless the act is so transparently self-serving as to backfire, negating the "generosity factor" and embarrassing the donor).

The image of Microsoft has always been very closely identified with the image of its founder. In marketing terms, this is a double-edged sword. Bill Gates claims to have long believed that one day personal computers would be on every desktop and in every home. If people approve of Gates and what he represents, there's a good chance they will like his company. People who *dislike*, resent, envy, or dismiss Gates dislike the company. Such a state of affairs can be dangerous if an influential industry publication's editor, a writer, or a legislator is the person doing the disliking.

For the brand to address this concern, one strategy demands distancing the person (Gates) from the product or brand (Microsoft). It is not necessary to hide him or to pretend he doesn't exist; a founder, after all, *is* still a founder. He might continue in the role of CEO, give interviews on occasion, but bring forward other executives and designate particular people as company spokespersons. The brand's identification and appeal, or lack thereof, will not be centered around Gates and the perception of him or his personality.

Sometimes a brand is so large and visible that it seems to overwhelm the product—and the customer. Microsoft was on its way to becoming such a brand. Ads such as this one sought to personalize the brand and make it seem more at the service of the customer and system, not the other way around. It's a good approach that should have been introduced earlier in order to be most effective.

Microsoft is a registered trademark of Microsoft Corporation.

It rarely takes long for market leaders to recognize that they have hit the bull's-eye or are the fastest gun in town that everyone wants to try to outdraw. The smartest market leaders learn early on that it is enough to be what they are, and good business sense demands that they lower their profile. Indeed, by the time the company introduced Windows 98, the dramatic fanfare of its predecessor version was still resonating. Microsoft wisely brought the product to market with less drumbeating and an appropriately lowered sense of anticipation. It was not advertised as the event of the century.

Microsoft, however, had momentum in its favor with Windows 95. The fastest-growing company in the nation's fastest-growing industry could not resist raising its voice to be heard from the top of the mountain. Alas, the time was one in which the greatest amount of attention was paid to innovation, imagination, . . . and *litigation.*

Competitors pursued market share by suing Microsoft, claiming it had engaged in heavy-handed tactics to dominate the market. The U.S. Justice Department was suing the company as well, largely for the same reasons.

Without trying to judge the merits of such actions, it should be noted that Microsoft listened to the market and responded. It had more than earned its market share; it had helped create the very market itself. It dominated the market. Was the domination through unfair practices or through carefully reacting to the mood of the market and aggressively ensuring the availability of its products as promised? Was it simply being *competitive?*

Gates responded to critics in interviews, through press spokespersons, and later by signing an "open letter" that appeared in national newspapers. It read:

To Our Customers, Partners, and Shareholders:

When Microsoft was formed 23 years ago, we made a commitment to innovation—to creating software that would bring the benefits of affordable, accessible computing into every home and office. Today, PCs are helping people be more productive at work, helping children learn and get access to the Internet at school, and helping families communicate with each other. This is an industry built on innovation, competition, and consumer choice—principles that America's antitrust laws were designed to promote, and that have always been a cornerstone of Microsoft's business practices.

Yet, as you may have heard, on May 18th the Department of Justice and a number of state Attorneys General filed antitrust lawsuits against us in federal court. We believe that the allegations made in these lawsuits are without merit—and the litigation, if it were to succeed, would hurt consumers and high-tech companies everywhere, not to mention the U.S. economy. . . .

. . . Without the ability to create and improve new products, no high-tech company could survive—and consumers everywhere will be worse off.

Sincerely,
Bill Gates

One day after the "open letter" ad appeared in the *New York Times*, that paper wrote, "The Government's antitrust case against Microsoft Corporation is shaping up as a high-decibel, often nasty battle to sway public opinion as well as the courts."

No kidding.

As has been noted, no brand compares itself to Brand X in its advertising anymore; it attacks the competitor head on, by name, in full frontal assault. And the brand that has been attacked will often respond in kind, retaliating against its competitor and trying to "one-up" the attack. Check the advertising of AT&T, GTE Sprint, MCI, and almost every other long-distance phone service for the most dramatic examples of this. "The Pepsi Challenge" didn't take on Brand X; it went after Coca-Cola—by name and with its logo right out front.

Marketers understand, as do lawyers, that most cases *are* ultimately won in the court of public opinion, but Microsoft's concern must be not only with its *legal* outcome, but with the preservation of its reputation, integrity, and brand equity.

In the modern marketing environment, one must take the pulse of public opinion, even with matters that seem as black-and-white as what might be a violation of laws. On the day Bill Gates's "open letter" appeared in the *New York Times*, the company's troubles were being covered on the front page of the newspaper's business section. Under a headline, "A Goliath Needs the Little Guys—Microsoft Faces Challenge of Image Among Consumers," an accountant's quote was typical of sentiments being offered: "We should be happy to have a great American company like Microsoft. The products have been great and the price has been right. The Government shouldn't blow a whistle just because it's a success."

What? An upstanding member of the public actually suggesting that, even if laws were violated, the company should get a pass because people like them and their products? Ignore the law? Perhaps another time, in another era, a hanging judge would be encouraged to throw the book at such a company. But in modern times, the public has been more inclined to focus on the spirit, rather than the letter of the law. If a person or product does not appear to be *all that bad* and his or its other contributions appear to outweigh the offense in question, it's OK.

This is not to suggest that marketers should try to advance their products or brands by being devious. It is, however, taking note that success comes to those who listen to the voice of the market and give the people what they want, even if the company's tactics may sometimes seem a bit heavy-handed.

✤ Physicians live by the words of Hippocrates, "First, do no harm." Any marketer who demonstrates a desire to accommodate the public without "doing harm" will very likely win support, goodwill, and loyalty. A company with a brand that becomes synonymous with good quality, price, service, value, and image will find a forgiving and supportive public. Taking such a "Robin Hood" approach to doing business is pretty risky, however.

Brand marketers should be both honest and honorable. It is entirely possible, even in the worst of times, to do extremely well with a good product that is well priced and well positioned. Microsoft's troubles occurred as the very successful company was still relatively young. Older, vastly more experienced and established companies are sued all the time, often by competitors and just as often by the government or regulators.

Whatever the facts are in a legal case, the company must continue to advertise, market, and make its case for the brand's USP (unique selling proposition) and its value to consumers. Being the industry leader does not lessen the need to continually reinforce that principle, particularly in so aggressively competitive and rapidly changing a market as that of personal computer technology.

As to the issue of separating the image of Bill Gates from the image of the products and brand, a parallel campaign would be most effective, neither neglecting the brand nor the person responsible for its past, present, and future.

The company appeared to have taken such an approach in offering the youthful CEO for speaking engagements and interviews, while brand marketing continued. Some critics have suggested that reported threats against Gates, a well-photographed episode in which he received a pie in the face, and demonstrating to TV's Barbara Walters how he sings a lullaby to his baby daughter were staged to soften his image when the company was being sued. Public cynicism was what the company experienced at the time. While no evidence is apparent to support accusations of "staged" incidents, it must be noted that it is certainly possible, but it would not be the first time critics tried to dismiss or discredit evidence that might evoke sympathy for an adversary.

Contrary to the old adage that "Any publicity is good publicity," Microsoft could do without lawsuits and competitive attacks. But such occurrences "come with the territory" of being number one. A continued emphasis on price, quality, and overall value is likely to keep the brand number one for some time to come.

Selling the Brand from the Inside Out: Intel

Intel Corporation is America's most successful producer of processors for computers. The company generates a huge amount of print and television advertising (like pharmaceutical companies advertising on the Sunday morning news shows, all of this is aimed at influencing legislators, regulators, and members of the financial community more than the general public).

Again, the computer industry is still in its relative infancy. As such, advertising for this industry's products is still "feeling its way along." Not that long ago, the earliest ads for computers all pictured the product, which basically looked like a large metal box. The metal boxes of one company looked a great deal like the metal boxes of every other.

As the product became more refined and more sophisticated, it became smaller. Most ads began focusing on what the computers could *do* and less on how they *looked*. Ads for computers then began to look like the ads for copy machines, life insurance, banks, and Sheraton hotels. Suffice it to say the market was maturing.

The mass audience pretty much knows two things about computers: there is *hardware,* as provided by companies such as IBM, and there is *software,* as developed by Microsoft and others. Beyond that, techies are free to learn the language and every nuance associated with the product; most people seem content (as with their automobiles) to simply *use* the product without really taking a great interest in how it works.

So what makes a good computer ad, and how does this affect the Intel brand?

There has always been a school of marketing that teaches the following: *never mind the jingles and pictures and lists of benefits, just be "out there" all the time advertising, and the competition will be left in the dust.*

When dealing with people who take this no-nonsense, no-frills approach, it is a good idea to read the fine print on the product's label. It's certainly appropriate to be brief and concise and to not distract the consumer with a lot of "glitz overkill." But while a barrage of message-free, benefit-free advertising might very well create awareness, it will do little to build brand equity, brand loyalty, or a reputation that can be rich enough to spread to other ventures. The best ads highlight the USP (unique selling proposition) and list the benefits and advantages to the consumer.

Still, the "never mind what you say—just advertise" approach has succeeded enough times to keep the form alive. Its supporters insist that a successful end result means the approach is effective, and no amount of marketing theory will alter that. Consider that a free sample will get someone to *try* a product but will not ensure a future purchase. A coupon for free or discounted merchandise will provide an incentive to try it but will not create a bond to purchase again. It is the customer's understanding and appreciation of the value in the product that creates brand loyalty and, from that, brand equity.

P. J. Cullerton was a great example of the success of

So, you say you're in the market for a new microprocessor? Huh? While the customer was being asked to look for the label that read "Intel inside," it was really Wall Street that the label was talking to. Although the customer knew little of the quality characteristics of microprocessors, a perception of brand quality made the Intel label a selling point for computers, and the perceived quality made Intel stock look good to security analysts.

Ad copyright © 1998 Intel Corporation.

this approach to advertising. The man was ʔ
ran for Cook County (Illinois) assessor anᵈ
the office term after term for years. Yet no ᴜ.
remember what he looked like or what position ꜟᵤ
on issues that concerned the voters. Year after year, he
bought billboard space in the most strategic locations. The
billboards read "Elect P. J. Cullerton Cook County Assessor." As election time neared, volunteers on street corners
and at shopping centers distributed shopping bags by the
tens of thousands. The paper bags had printed on them, in
the same type style and color as the billboards, "Elect P. J.
Cullerton Cook County Assessor."

When Cullerton passed away, his photo appeared next
to his obituary, prompting people to say, "So *that's* what he
looked like."

Admittedly, the position of county assessor is not the
high-profile job that is typically marked with rigorous
debate, but the point is, Cullerton counted on the billboards and shopping bags to create a high degree of
name recognition. As people entered their voting booths
the recognition and familiarity of his name would register favorably. The strategy worked successfully for years,
despite the urging of political operatives who would have
preferred the candidate to be more "out front."

Similarly, Intel Corporation, in all its print ads and
television commercials, makes no attempt to explain how
a "processor" or a "microprocessor" or even a "computer
chip" works—or even what it *is*. The company apparently
takes the view that its objective is to promote the *brand*,
not knowledge of the internal workings of a computer,
and that is certainly a legitimate point. The ads are full
pages or more, often in color, in the largest circulation
publications in the world, in both the financial and general interest media. They appear often.

Some marketers would take the view that "saturation
advertising" is hardly a creative approach to building brand
awareness, even though it very often works.

"Today, repetition is equated with importance but disconnected from excellence," notes Edwin Schlossberg. "In the past, high visibility of an idea could be interpreted as an expression on the part of cultural leaders and others that this idea, this person, or this thing was important for all of us."

More important, every computer that uses an Intel processor displays a miniature decal with the company's logo on both its casing and packaging. Just as the public is conditioned to react positively when it sees that a food product is "made with real Hershey's chocolate," the public, government regulators, legislators, and Wall Street brokers are being programmed to read that a computer has something special going for it if it includes the Intel pentium processor.

Most people don't know what the pentium processor is, but indications are that they think it's something good. In terms of brand equity, it is by a very comfortable margin the *only* brand of processor people know.

It may not be particularly educational or benefit-oriented, but as a brand strategy, it works.

Sex Sells . . . Sometimes: Playboy

Playboy is a brand name rich in imagery, symbolizing more than the magazine from which a publicly traded empire grew. While its tremendous popularity and success shocked many people, it shouldn't have. It was a classic case of giving the public what it wanted and packaging it tastefully enough that people who might normally have been uncomfortable with the product's content could accept it as sophisticated and even tasteful.

Playboy, as a publication, redefined the men's magazine category by combining photographs of beautiful women with a high level of quality in everything else within its pages. Many of the world's best-known contemporary fiction writers, essayists, and sports journalists were presented along with interviews with world leaders and deep thinkers. Even the ads in the publication were elegant and sophisticated. Early ads promoting the magazine asked in their headlines, "What sort of man reads *Playboy*?"

The answer, it was suggested, was youthful yet mature. He was a literate lover of the good life—one who could afford to live it or certainly aspire to it. This was a classic variation on the old advertising question "Can you see yourself in this picture?" In *Playboy*'s case, the young male audience most definitely wanted to.

The magazine succeeded from its very start, achieving a respectability in a magazine category that literally had none. This was not just another men's magazine with stories about cars and photos of beautiful nude women. *Playboy* was a philosophical manifesto.

But sometimes achieving great success can cause a personal or corporate compass to go haywire, causing a feeling that there is such a thing as a "golden touch."

Between branded products and licensing deals with a broad range of ventures in between, Playboy Enterprises learned the expensive lesson that everything to which it affixed the Playboy name (and attached the *Playboy* persona) did not automatically succeed.

Playboy founder, editor, and publisher, Hugh Hefner, articulated and sought to embody the "Playboy Philosophy" in his writings and lifestyle. Following the success of his magazine, he served as host of a television show, *Playboy's Penthouse,* and later *Playboy After Dark.*

While awkward and often silly in their staged, party atmosphere, the TV programs tried to bring to life the glamour and sophistication that were so much a part of the magazine. This launched the beginning of *Playboy*'s brand extensions. Hefner attempted to put the name he now thought represented a way of life and personal philosophy on a range of products, including a worldwide chain of Playboy Clubs, members-only nightclubs featuring the top entertainers of the world; a book publishing company, Playboy Press, offering upscale and high-priced books on censorship, music, and wine and even *The Playboy Illustrated History of Organized Crime*; a record label, Playboy Records, that specialized in jazz and country music; and even a chain of Playboy Hotels and Resorts.

These products, from magazines to hotels, could be considered brand extensions because they used the same name and sought to capitalize on the same image and brand identification in the marketplace. They also operated fully under the same ownership and management that distinguishes them as extensions, not licenses.

Licensing was a separate area and one that Hefner exploited mightily in lucrative deals that put the Playboy name and rabbit-head symbol on clothing, jewelry, glassware, and a plethora of other merchandise including automobile air fresheners.

While some products and ventures were more successful than others, the public didn't scrutinize the business side of the matter, because it was, after all, Hefner's money at the time (the company was still privately held). If he chose to indulge himself by being a publisher/record mogul/hotelier/nightclub owner, whose business was it?

Any notorious public misstep eventually becomes the stuff of gossipy rise-and-fall legends. Hugh Hefner was no exception. He was a character much larger than life as spokesman and head of the empire he created, but in time the ears on the Playboy bunny began to droop, along with the company's revenue.

A couple of things happened.

The first was the sexual revolution. The 1970s were marked by an atmosphere of openness and a more liberal attitude toward sex and sexuality. Nudity seemed acceptable, even routine, in Hollywood films. Serious national news magazines reflected the style exemplified by trendy "encounter groups" where people openly shared their most intimate thoughts. There were bars and fashions whose names began with the word *topless* and even respectable clubs with entertainment that featured nude dancers. In the midst of all this, the *Playboy* image seemed suddenly out of date and out of touch. The famous "bunnies" of the Playboy Clubs looked dated, trussed up in harness-like skimpy outfits with rabbit ears and tails.

The new urban sophisticates were not just the "sort of man who reads *Playboy*," but men of very diverse interests, and a lot of outspoken, assertive women as well.

The flagship magazine's circulation and ad sales declined dramatically, and the clubs (still "members only") fell on hard times, out of place in the prevailing environment.

The second problem was that the smooth, smirking image associated with the term *playboy* played fine in the early 1960s, but with the rise of feminism among women and consciousness-raising among men, the clubs and hotels were vastly out of step with the market. Few women felt comfortable in a club where waitresses dressed as "bunnies." Many businesses took a dim view of finding "Playboy Hotel," with its frivolous connotation, listed on an expense report.

The golden brand seemed laden with rust.

While some companies that build a brand on image hold that image as sacred and refuse to compromise, Hugh Hefner and his directors (the company by now was publicly traded) knew that if any equity in the Playboy name was to remain, changes had to be made. Hefner, while retaining the title of chairman, all but retired to his California estate and left his very bright, equally image-conscious daughter running the company. A team of business professionals closed the clubs and sold or renamed the hotels. The record company and book publishing operations disappearing. A film production company, after several disappointing big-budget features, began concentrating on more modestly budgeted home video projects and programming for the company's cable TV channel.

If a market observer were to conclude that Playboy had stumbled, it would be for these reasons:

1. It failed to check the pulse of the market regularly to see if it was still giving the public what it wanted.

2. It assumed the power of the Playboy name would be enough to carry it as the company diversified into areas that had little or nothing to do with the unique selling proposition upon which the company's original success was based.

3. It grossly miscalculated, failing to understand that just because a magazine built around pictures of beautiful women and good writing is a success, it doesn't naturally follow that a record company or hotel will be a success because the same guy owns it.

By the 1990s, *Playboy* was again doing well. The magazine was profitable and seemed to accept that it was a literate, sexy men's magazine and not a philosophy of life. This time *Playboy* brand extensions were calendars that reflected the content of the magazine, single subject "collector's edition" magazines (outtakes from the original magazine pictorials), games, and jigsaw puzzles. The company had become very successful in home videos that are video adaptations of the magazine's content, as is much of the programming on the cable TV channel.

Playboy Enterprises remains determined to exploit its name and logo to the greatest extent possible. To best accomplish this, there is a mail-order catalog and a computer website. The catalog, *Playboy Products for Good Times*, offers videos, lingerie, jewelry, books, back issues of the magazine, and other merchandise. The Playboy website offers material matching the content of the magazine and the catalog for people who prefer to turn their pages electronically.

Although there is a good deal of money to be made in automobile air fresheners, Playboy appears to have returned to its core business of publishing a magazine and not straying far afield when it wants to offer more.

Playboy stood out as a magazine because it was different. It was political, topical, and issue-oriented in ways that the news weeklies and intellectual journals were not; it was sexy, an escapist vision of flesh and fantasy, in ways the sleazy "girlie" magazines were not. The sexy part was what people seemed to notice and appreciate most. These political, topical, sexy, and fantasy elements were not easily transferable nor affordable, so most of the other businesses where Playboy tried to expand were not successful.

The fantasy element was key. Reading the magazine, viewing the Playboy Channel, checking the website, and watching the videos, the reader/viewer can afford to indulge in the "What sort of man reads *Playboy*? Can you see yourself in this picture?" daydream, fantasy, and aspiration. Going to a club or a hotel removes the element of fantasy and demands full participation at a substantial price.

Research would have told Playboy that for its target market (the sort of man who reads *Playboy*), sex still sells, but not at any price.

Sometimes a Brand Can "Just Do It" Too Much: Nike

In many ways, it was a repeat of the Playboy experience, except in this case the clothes were being put *on*. Nike marked its 25th anniversary in 1997 with an extra reason to celebrate. The company was just completing the most financially successful 12 months in its history. Its logo, described as looking like a cross between a check mark and a boomerang, referred to as a "swoosh," was considered to be one of the most recognizable logos throughout the world, some say second only to that of Coca-Cola.

A year later, the world's leading maker of athletic shoes and apparel reported record sales of $9.6 billion, but a 49 percent drop in profits and a 50 percent decline in its stock price from its highs of a year earlier.

Ouch!

It was a fascinating turn, by marketing standards. A company that had taken such a huge financial hit in a year's time should have hit the wall, crashed and burned, and probably racked up at least two additional clichés synonymous with disaster, but Nike, uh, . . . kept running. Worldwide, the company has about half the total market in athletic shoes.

"Nike was a marketing MVP. But with its image, brand, and business under fire, a company and a CEO with a sense of mission are suddenly reeling," reported *Newsweek.*

Warehouses were full of shoes that weren't selling. The company's critics, especially human rights organizations all over the world, were increasing pressure on Nike for its notorious use of cheap labor, particularly in its factories in Indonesia.

The *New York Times Magazine* described the situation as, "The coolest kids think the logo means 'uncool.' Liberals think it means 'exploits Asian workers.' Has branding given Nike a bad name?"

The question is an interesting one. Starting with a product that the world simply dismissed as "sneakers," Nike rolled over such powerful competitors as Reebok and Adidas, positioning its brand as the preeminent designer label and identifying itself with the greatest names of the day in sports, including basketball legend Michael Jordan, baseball great Ken Griffey Jr., and tennis star John McEnroe, among others. (Jordan has successfully become a "brand within a brand," with his own logo bumping the "swoosh" off the line products he endorses for Nike.)

"The greatest secret of the sports-footwear-and-apparel business," Timothy Egan wrote, "is that most of the product is bought by people who want to be like Mike or Ken Griffey Jr. or the Brazilian soccer star Renaldo, but seldom leave the couch."

"The reason the basketball shoes have worked so well is because 80 percent of the people who buy them never set foot on a basketball court—it's a fashion statement," said footwear industry analyst Vince Francom, noting, "The problem with fashion is that tastes change very quickly. There's a big backlash against Nike under way. The skateboard generation doesn't want to wear Nikes because their fathers wear them."

The company's cofounder and CEO Philip Knight believed that much of the problem stemmed from "too much visibility."

Indeed. The victim in a school shooting incident wore clothing described as "covered in Nike logos." Former football great O. J. Simpson, best remembered as the defendant in a gruesome double-murder case, posed for photographs while wearing a Nike cap.

While this company began humbly, it purchased its market share over a dozen years of celebrity-studded saturation advertising. Largely having built its reputation as the brand of the top talent in athletics by purchasing their endorsements, Nike can sustain its billions of dollars in annual sales by either dumb luck or a marketing strategy that takes notice of its areas of vulnerability.

If the company is criticized for being the fantasy brand of young poor kids, while selling shoes at an average price of $140 per pair, the problem needs to be fixed. A more affordable budget line can be offered. Grants can be made; shoes can be donated. If critics attack the company's use of cheap foreign labor, corrective measures can be taken. A company with more than $9 billion in annual sales can afford to offer domestic customers a product manufactured in the United States and let the cheaper products go out to the countries where prices are commensurate with the cost of manufacturing.

Nike's best-known ad slogan is "Just do it!" So . . . do good deeds. Nike can continue its sponsorships of leagues and teams and add to it by donating large blocks of tickets to schools and athletic programs that could not afford them otherwise. Scholarships are a way to get positive attention. The first rule of effective crisis management is, *don't let the first thing people know about you be negative news.*

These recommendations cost money and most certainly cut into company profits. But the course that Nike followed to find itself in trouble can be a costly one as well. A heavy ad rotation and high visibility for the brand name will most certainly result in sales. But the Nike brand is also a *franchise* that must be protected. Just racking up sales is not enough. The ability to maintain and exploit the brand into lines of clothing and other merchandise, as well as related sports equipment, is a bigger issue with higher stakes.

A high-profile, successful brand that does not position itself to correct its obvious problems and engender goodwill from its customer base is playing Russian roulette with its future. There are better games Nike could be playing.

An Exclusive Club for Almost Everyone: American Express

It is possible for brands to be launched and become "overnight sensations." A spectacular television moment, a great mail promotion, a sign held up at the Super Bowl— anything's possible. But most truly successful brands were not overnight sensations. Most have had the luxury of being introduced and having time to build with new products, acquisitions, and reinvestment of their profits in their own growth. Suddenly one day, people look around and it seems the brand name is everywhere and people can't remember when it wasn't. American Express is such a brand.

Like Playboy, American Express is a brand that is often not thought of as a brand, but rather as a company, a very large company involved in numerous businesses, including banking, brokerage, travel, mutual funds, investments, publishing, and technology. In some cases, one must squint to find the American Express identification, so discreet is its involvement. In other cases, like an important movie star, the company proudly splashes its name above the title of its operating divisions and events it rises to sponsor.

Some might conclude the company is out to impress its shareholders and the public by identifying itself with its most successful and highly visible endeavors, while downplaying its association with its less-profitable, more controversial ventures.

The American Express green card and American Express Travelers Cheques have brought the brand high visibility and prestige as well as significant revenue. Brand extensions such as the American Express gold card and travel services have substantially enhanced both the company's image and profits. Indeed, after a hefty decline in revenues during the 1980s, the company entered the '90s with nearly $10 billion in revenues from its travel-related businesses alone.

Some security analysts considered American Express's two brand extensions, the platinum card (going the gold card one better) and the Optima card (to compete with rival bankcards Mastercard and Visa), to be preordained successes. But both introductions fell well below expectations, causing financial and public relations embarrassment to the firm.

The platinum card was ill-conceived from the start.

Even the more snobbish prospects for this product dismissed the card as so overtly, embarrassingly, class conscious that one could not even apply for it but had to wait to be invited to receive it. Then they had to pay a stiff annual fee for the privilege of using it. And the Queen will be coming for tea. A problem with offering an elitist product is that

- the upscale market has so many choices that the inherent value in the product must be outstanding and immediately recognizable;

- people at the lower end of the market resent the very existence of a product that blatantly reminds them that they are not good enough to have it; and

- in most economic times, such an item appears to be more of an irrelevant indulgence that offers far more to the issuer than to the recipient.

Granted, the gold card was a big success and carried a suggestion of status. And granted, as more gold cards came into circulation, with banks offering their own versions (often at much lower fees) the snob appeal diminished. But the case for the platinum card was a weak one. It was lacking in significant benefits and launched in a depressed economic cycle. It sank of its own weight. There are in fact platinum cards issued, but as an item with the intent of being an impressive symbol of success, it never caught on.

One would have expected that American Express, with all its resources, would have learned from even the most superficial research that it was offering a product the marketplace did not want or need. What publicity the platinum card received was laced with ridicule.

The Optima card was another, but different, type of failure, equally unjustifiable given the talent and resources of American Express. For years, American Express, Diners' Club, and Carte Blanche owned the charge card business. Customers (or *members*, as the companies preferred to call them) paid an annual fee and paid account balances in full each month.

When the banks entered the business, they ultimately consolidated a myriad of labels under the banners Visa and Mastercard. They employed the revolving charge system, by which customers could pay installments on their balances each month, plus interest charges, and a smaller (if any) annual fee than was typically assessed by the big three.

Given the huge number of banks sending unsolicited cards to their customers, it was only a matter of time before those customers asked why they needed the more costly three cards when the bankcards were cheaper and more accessible. American Express's share of the U.S. general-purpose charge card business in the 1980s was 25 percent. By 1990, it had declined to 22.3 percent, and only a year later, to 20.6 percent, according to a report by *Advertising Age*. Clearly, the impact of bankcards was being felt.

So, where did American Express, one of America's true "power brands" fumble?

First, the company failed to see the signs of trouble brewing. In the late 1980s, the U.S. economy was in recession and concern about the cost of credit was rising. Merchants began complaining about (and refusing to honor) American Express cards because the merchant-paid service fees were much higher than those of its competitors. The issue reached an extreme when a group of Boston merchants actually organized a boycott of the company, with accompanying national news coverage.

Not only did American Express not budge on its service charges to merchants, but it continued to charge its members fees that were double or triple the annual fees of Visa or Mastercard participating banks.

During this same period, Sears introduced the Discover Card, yet another addition to the charge card derby, and its only success in a long list of corporate misjudgments. Discover Card was rolled out with massive advertising and publicity support. It was positioned as versatile, highly benefit-weighted, and value-oriented.

Both Visa and Mastercard increased their advertising, and Visa launched a frontal assault, noting places of interest that welcomed the Visa card but would not accept American Express.

The American Express reaction was somewhere between arrogant and ineffectual. The company scored well over the years with friendly, memorable, effective advertising campaigns, such as one using big-name celebrities with unfamiliar faces asking, "Do you know me?" or actor Karl Malden sounding the alarm for American Express Travelers Cheques ("Don't leave home without them"). American Express didn't seem inclined to dignify competitors' taunts with a response.

A very expensive American Express ad during this period merely showed very famous people in elegant portrait photographs, noting their names and how many years they had been American Express members.

Suggesting that the most compelling reason why people should get an American Express card was because Paul Newman, Wilt Chamberlain, and Rob Reiner had one wasn't much of an argument, especially when competitors were offering cost savings and convenience. A more dramatic, "feel good" message might have emphasized customers' peace of mind from knowing that a company with the strength and resources of American Express was behind them when they needed to pay and didn't have the cash at hand. The brand message, again, should be about *value to the customer.*

If the Optima card was to go head-to-head with bankcards, someone should have told the Optima people. An Optima ad program seemed to be saying that people should want an Optima card because it was from American Express. Cost advantages were not apparent. Promotion was heavily aimed at American Express customers (members) via direct mail solicitations, thus potentially cannibalizing the core product instead of focusing on new converts.

Further, merchants did not respond to Optima with nearly the enthusiasm shown for the introduction of the Discover Card or a new Visa. Where was American Express's research? Where was the unique selling proposition?

What about discounts, rebates, low interest rates, and a warm, inviting message instead of a detached suggestion that the company probably didn't need your business?

Enormous competitive pressure arose from General Motors, General Electric, Ford, and AT&T, each promoting their respective entry into the charge card business with customized Visa and Mastercards, with widely advertised special discounts and savings. American Express needed to respond.

The brand's next unsuccessful campaign was an extension of its theme of snobbery—a message that might well have been suited to the Victorian age, with the motto "Membership has its privileges."

According to *Advertising Age*, American Express committed a budget of $1.1 billion to marketing in a single year. Marketers were advocating a more creative, less pompous approach with a greater emphasis on value to the customer. The company needed to reenergize its sagging core products, the green card and traveler's checks, while defining "added value" for the Optima card and travel services.

Maybe.

Even in a rebound economy, consumers and merchants were reluctant to pay higher fees for the privilege of having an American Express card. If the campaign was intended to be tongue-in-cheek, no one seemed to get the joke.

American Express, a fine organization rich with intelligence, chose the wrong message for the social and economic climate in which it was supposed to be making a competitive stand. Survival, much less growth, of a company or a brand depends on its ability to maintain a competitive fee structure and a message that speaks to value, not just status.

A misstep for American Express was more serious than it might have been for Sears's Discover Card, because American Express's business is financial services—investing and managing money. American Express should have taken better care of how it handled its own financial dealings while the whole world was watching.

In many ways, American Express has grown by innovation, but it has also added to its considerable size through some very public acquisitions in the area of investment and brokerage.

IDS, founded in 1894 as Investors Diversified Services, was a Minneapolis-based firm that had built an excellent national reputation, especially in mutual funds, before it was acquired by American Express in 1984. Well-managed and with a public spirit, it was American Express's most profitable division throughout the early 1990s. Its posted assets under management were more than $65 billion, according to *Business Week*. While basking in the glow of such a fine public image, American Express announced in 1993 that it would spend about $1 billion to redesign the operation and would rename it American Express Personal Financial Planning.

Consider the backdrop against which the wisdom of this move might be judged:

1. In the view of Wall Street analysts, American Express had blundered a few times, lost an enormous amount of money, and appeared to be a falling star.
2. IDS had an excellent reputation among members of the financial services industry and the public.
3. American Express was spending an enormous amount of money to dismantle and reconfigure a well-regarded brand and blend it into one that seemed to be slipping.

The company might have done better to have launched a high-profile ad campaign that proudly identified American Express with IDS—a bit of the parent beaming with pride at a successful child—with a simple legend such as "IDS, an American Express Company." It could have savored the image of quality its acquired brand generated.

Instead, the company sped off in the opposite direction. Having acquired the brokerage firm of Shearson Hayden Stone in the 1970s, the company changed the name to Shearson American Express. Upon acquiring the investment banking firm of Lehman Brothers, the name was changed again, first to Shearson Lehman American Express, then just to Shearson Lehman. The investment banking unit operated as Lehman Brothers, with no reference whatsoever to American Express in its ads—even in the legal fine print copyright information. By early 1993, executives of American Express were talking openly about unloading the entire brokerage division and had courted potential buyers in full public view.

A reasonable person might have concluded that American Express wanted to identify itself prominently with the success and good name earned by IDS and to distance itself from the risky, high-profile investment banking activities of Lehman Brothers. Alas, the message it was sending openly to its shareholders, security analysts, and the general public was a picture of a rudderless ship.

Much less known is the American Express experience with publishing. In the early 1990s, the company owned and published the magazines *Travel & Leisure*, *Food & Wine*, *L.A. Style*, *D.*, and *Atlanta*. If the company wanted to position itself as the investment group that it was, rather than as a magazine publisher, that was OK. In less than a year, management control of the magazines passed from American Express to Time Warner.

If American Express had a plan to manage its brand, it was a hazy one indeed. Marketers wondered why, with all its resources and capabilities, the company appeared so unfocused, disorganized, and wasteful of the equity in a great franchise.

An operation the size of American Express can, of course, run as many companies as it chooses under separate names. They *should*, however, all be identified with the legend "An American Express Company" if the brand is to maintain the integrity of its trademark. Or, the companies should all have names that take second place to the parent (such as *American Express Food & Wine*, American Express IDS Personal Finance, American Express Lehman Brothers, etc.). A company cannot successfully maximize the value of its brand name if it shades or altogether hides that brand name.

American Airlines had a great idea: hook up with a major credit card company and offer "mileage points" on American every time the card is used. Credit card usage is encouraged because there's a bonus payback to the consumer in the form of free flights, upgrades, and whatever kind of point redemption program the card issuers can come up with.

Executives of American Airlines thought the name identification with American Express made the combination a natural. Except for one small problem: American Express chose to pass on the deal. American Airlines then took the idea to Citibank, which issued, at the customer's choice, either a Visa card or a Mastercard (or both) carrying the joint logos of Citibank and American Airlines. The card program was designated Citibank AAdvantage and proved to be a huge success, with tens of thousands of cards issued and usage running at an impressively high level.

It took a while for American Express to acknowledge that it was embarrassed by screwing up the airline partnership, another very public misjudgment. Trying to recover, the company approached Delta Airlines, made a deal, and issued a joint card with mileage points—the

Delta Sky Miles Card from American Express. While not a complete disaster, it was a very pale and distant imitation of the Citibank AAdvantage card and didn't nearly approach its success.

A repositioning of the American Express Optima Card as the Optima True Grace card was a try at introducing a touch of humility and an expression of gratitude to customers. It was regarded as too little, too late. New American Express Corporate Cards were issued with a huge (and somewhat confused and unfocused) advertising and promotional effort, along with a pitch for American Express Small Business Services. The company seemed to be saying that this time it really wanted to help its customers. *Really.*

Again, the success was marginal. The public didn't quite get what "true grace" meant, and it wasn't clear that the company knew either. The effort was received better than the arrogant "Membership has its privileges" message. However, American Express had put itself on a level with the post office and the phone company—so huge and sprawling that a public announcement of caring about the kind of service it provided was received with a guffaw from a disbelieving public.

The public and the market are historically forgiving. If American Express "has its act together," a major public relations initiative should spell out things the company is doing correctly in newspaper and magazine "advertorials" and should be highly visible to the public, creating a public record of service. Mobil Oil Corporation used exactly this approach during the oil industry crisis in America. The result was that Mobil won respect and recognition for its candor, integrity, and strength. Mobil also put its name on a huge grant to PBS and other public service works. The public knew the gifts were self-serving, but that was OK because the subsidies were real and the benefits to the arts and the public were visible.

American Express, as a company and as a brand, should be committed to enhancing the intrinsic value of its name. The marketplace will tell if and when it reaches a point of diminishing returns. The company and the brand need to be represented to its public as more than simply big and self-important if it is to take advantage of opportunities and maintain its brand equity. As confusion spreads, American Express may appear in one of its own ads, asking the audience, "Do you know me?"

Big Wheels from Out of Town

Honda

Some marketers have suggested that Honda's experience in the U.S. market is an example of need catching up with a product.

When Honda made its American debut, it was as a motorcycle, a *small* motorcycle at that. Until that time, Americans had related to motorcycles as heavy, powerful machines, typified by Harley-Davidson products. Motorcycles were no-nonsense machines ridden by state troopers. But Honda's motorcycles, like similar models by other Japanese manufacturers such as Suzuki and Yamaha, were lightweight, smaller, economical to maintain, and easy to handle. They were also relatively inexpensive.

A significant distinction comes into play at this point: for years Japan's exported products, from radios to copiers, had been pretty much dismissed as cheap (cheaply made and cheap to buy). Certainly the message, not totally a burst of nationalism, was that these "made in Japan" brands were vastly inferior to "American made" products.

Honda, along with Sony, Panasonic, and a few others, changed the way Americans thought of Japanese-made products.

As provincial as the American consumer chose to be at times, grudging recognition was given to the fact that this new generation of Japanese products, particularly motor vehicles and electronics, was equal to or better than their American-made counterparts. Quality and technology were up and cost was down. The moral argument of one company (or country) using "cheap labor" versus another using "skilled union workers" was a strong patriotic message. But when the time came to actually write the check, sales of Japanese products soared. The lesson for marketers was that consumers did not wish to have their patriotism challenged, but they also didn't want to pay more than what they perceived as a fair or competitive price for a quality product.

Honda became the motorcycle of choice for college and high school students in need of dependable, low-cost transportation. As environmental concerns increased and fuel economy became a greater issue, air pollution, avoiding traffic jams, and accessible parking became more important considerations—and selling points.

Before long, thousands of younger American men and women, like their European counterparts, began riding these lightweight motorcycles to and from work, recognizing a more fuel-efficient, less expensive alternative to the automobile. The most popular of these motorcycles was the Honda—so popular it was the subject of a hit song, *Little Honda*, that topped record charts in 1964. As economical, basic transportation, the product had achieved clear niche respectability.

Then, Honda took an extremely bold step: the motorcycle company tried to sell Americans cars.

The initial response was dismissive. Suggestions were that the company was putting those little motorcycle tires on, well, little cars, and that it didn't deserve to be taken seriously. The price was small relative to the cost of an American-made car, which seemed to suggest Honda's car was another of Japan's "cheap" products. Then two things happened. First, the cars performed extremely well in terms of fuel efficiency, dependability, and maintenance. Second, there was a social trend shift that attacked the bigger, more expensive American "gas guzzlers" and embraced smaller, more economical cars.

Price, quality, and image equal value.

The Honda automobile tires got a little bigger and so did the passenger compartment. While in no danger of being mistaken for an Oldsmobile, Honda had fine-tuned its cars to the point that its Civic model became a top seller in America. It was a symbol of style, fuel efficiency, and good engineering.

If the brand extension leap from motorcycle to car wasn't impressive enough, in the 1980s Honda introduced Acura, a line of fine cars with features, appointments, and performance on a par with established luxury models. Although the company made no secret of its manufacturing role, the Honda name does not appear on the car or in its advertising, lest the customer have second thoughts about paying luxury car prices for... a Honda.

From motorcycle to economical family car to luxury car, Honda looked at what people wanted in transportation and created and sold products that met that need. A large product recall in 1998 did not hurt the brand's image at all. Novelist Kurt Vonnegut said in an interview that he drove a Honda Civic that was several years old at the time. Katie Couric, host of the top-rated NBC *Today Show*, casually mentioned in banter with her coanchor that she drove a 13-year-old Honda, despite earning several million dollars per year.

The impression of casual remarks such as these from well-regarded, wealthy people who influence others was that the brand represented quality and, despite its affordable price tag, they didn't need more than that.

The brand's advertising was consistent and focused, keeping prominent its profile and the product's benefits to the consumer. It was a simple formula approach and very successful.

Hyundai

In previous chapters, attention was given to the importance of choosing the right name for a product or brand, positioning it clearly, and focusing on achieving familiarity and recognition, so that the *brand power* of the core product can be profitably transferred to other products. Here Hyundai runs into trouble.

The brand entered the United States in 1986 with considerable fanfare, a large ad budget, and a compact car—the Hyundai Excel. Hyundai planned to buy market share if it had to, coming in strong and expecting to become a major force in the U.S. market fast. As news spread throughout the auto industry, the threat was taken very seriously.

It needn't have worried.

The company proved to be less effective at selling cars than it was at making waves. According to the trade publication *Automotive News*, Hyundai Motors America entered the 1990s with around 1 percent of U.S. car and light truck sales, having peaked in 1988 with some 264,000 units sold.

As compact cars go, both import and domestic, Hyundai had a respectable product in terms of quality, design, performance, and, above all, price. Its U.S. debut came when the country's auto industry leadership did nothing to discourage import-bashing, particularly disparaging cars made in Japan.

Hyundai cars are products of South Korea, but Hyundai made little effort to distance itself from popular Japanese imports (Honda, Toyota, Nissan, and Subaru), which were holding an increasingly large U.S. market share in spite of an aggressive "buy American" ad campaign.

Japanese and Korean imports were generally cheaper than or competitive with American cars and represented, in the minds of many people, a greater value in terms of performance, style, engineering, and quality. These considerations did much to blunt the swell of patriotic sentiment. American consumers apparently preferred to choose their battles. Clearly, some folks would always buy only American, but on such a big ticket item as an automobile, the typical consumer was more interested in value than dressing in the flag. Consumers candidly expressed a sentiment that Detroit had let them down. In such a climate, a new and considerably lower priced import should have done extremely well.

However

1. As the newest player in a crowded field, Hyundai had to work a lot harder and spend more for recognition.

2. The company found American consumers hesitant, lacking knowledge of South Korean products, and questioning how they did or didn't measure up to the popular Japanese cars, much less American cars.

3. Five years after entering the U.S. market, most people still could not pronounce, much less *spell* the name of the brand correctly. (*Hyundai* rhymes with *Sunday.*) Yet announcers, even in some of their own commercials, would pronounce it "high-yun-dye."

On the threshold of a new century, Hyundai remained serious about wanting to establish itself as a significant brand in the United States, but with a more modest share of the market than it might once have thought possible. As its identification with the compact family car market was building, the company introduced an upline model called Sonata, the sporty Scoupe, and the subcompact Elantra—three models with very differing levels of appeal. This was a questionable strategy for a brand that still needed to define itself.

But in the auto industry, having different models is a defensible position, despite the brand's youth. What was terribly odd was the decision to introduce Hyundai personal computers to the U.S. market at a time when auto buyers still weren't able to pronounce the brand's name.

One might expect that well-financed non-U.
panies would examine considerable research befo
entering each new market. Hyundai certainly had the
resources to do so, and its products could stand up well
under scrutiny. Yet Hyundai never really seemed to define
the USP (unique selling proposition) for its cars and did
so even less for its personal computers. Both were in the
low single digits in market share throughout the 1990s.
The marketer's message must give consumers a reason to
buy. It is not enough just to be there.

Hyundai could have distinguished itself by becoming
the official brand of something—the local dance troupe,
the film society, or the school band. Cars could have been
donated to help transport preschoolers or nursing home
residents.

College students could have been photographed study-
ing in them, eating dinner in them, making plans to save
the world in them, or seeing how many people wearing
white sweatshirts with the brand logo could fit inside one—
an idea similar to one that didn't hurt Volkswagon's early
quest for publicity.

To establish the brand in a highly competitive environment, any advertising is better than no advertising.
But if a company is going to pay for the advertising anyway, it should say more than "there are a lot of cars out
there and this is one of them." The consumer needs a
reason to favor one brand over another. A marketer's
challenge is to supply that reason.

The Candy Wars

Think of Valentine's Day, Mother's Day, Secretary's Day,
birthdays, anniversaries, and a little something for the host-
ess, and it's a good bet that candy comes to mind. Even
without a reason or a special occasion, candy is big business

—more than a $6.4 billion business, according to Nielsen Marketing Research and *Advertising Age*. In the 1990s Hershey Foods dominated the industry with a nearly 28 percent market share in the United States. Its closest competitor, Mars, Incorporated, had an almost 24 percent share. That these two companies sell about half the candy bought in America suggests their obvious power of production and distribution, but it also says they have a good sense of what keeps the country's sweet tooth sweet. The companies are intensely competitive, alert to not only the public's changing tastes, but convenience considerations—from "bite size" to "the big bag" family packs. As to status, Hershey's Golden Almond bar is chocolate in an elegant gold foil wrap, selling image as much as it's selling candy. And let's not forget Snickers's proud declaration that it had been "chosen" the Official Snack Food of the United States Olympic Team.

How many of America's favorite sweets are brands of Hershey Foods or Mars, Inc., and how intense is their effort to make every brand work harder? Consider the list below as a starting point. For purposes of illustration, the list is limited to major national confectionery brand products, and by the time you read this, it may be longer:

Hershey's at Your Candy Counter

Hershey's Milk Chocolate Bar	Reese's Peanut Butter Cups
Hershey's Milk Chocolate with Almonds	Reese's Crunchy Peanut Butter Cup
Hershey's Cookies and Mint	Reese's Crunchy Cookie Cup
Hershey's Cookies 'n' Creme	ReeseSticks
Hershey's Special Dark	Reese's Nutrageous
Hershey's Bites	Reese's Miniatures
Hershey's Big Block	Reese's Pieces
Hershey's Miniatures	Reese's Peanut Butter Puffs

Hershey's Kisses

Hershey's Hugs

Hershey's Giant Kiss

Hershey's Golden Almond
  Bar

Hershey's Mr. Goodbar

Hershey's Krackel Bar

Hershey's Golden Almond
  Solitaires

Hershey's Tastations Hard
  Candies

Mounds

Almond Joy

Whatchamacallit

Symphony Candy Bar

York Peppermint Pattie

KitKat Bar

Rolo

Caramels

Skor Toffee Bar

Mars Sweet Selections

M&M's Plain

M&M's Peanut

M&M's Almond

M&M's Peanut Butter

M&M's Crispy

Milky Way Candy Bar

Milky Way Dark

Milky Way Lite

Milky Way Milk Shakes

Milky Way Ice Cream Bars

PB Max

Mars Chocolate
  Almond

Twix

Snickers

Snickers Peanut Butter Bar

Snickers Ice Cream Bar

3 Musketeers

3 Musketeers Ice Cream Bar

Kudos

Holidays

Starburst

Skittles

Dove Chocolate Bars

Dove Ice Cream Bars

Hershey's

Some people might make the case that candy is responsible for fortunes being made in dentistry and medicine as well as in the snack food industry, but those are people who probably don't have much fun. Some people, of course, would argue that candy does not deserve to be called a "food."

The confectionery industry, large and powerful, even has its own trade association, the National Confectionery Association, and why shouldn't it, with the billions of dollars spent annually on candy? Perhaps the most popular candy is chocolate, and there are people who will proudly stand up and declare themselves "chocoholics." True chocolate lovers enjoy a vigorous debate on the merits of Swiss versus German chocolate, of Godiva versus the Hershey bar, and of regional favorites like San Francisco's Ghirardelli and Chicago's Fannie May.

The popularity of candy in its various forms may be traced back in history. Many of the great old films set around the time of World War II suggested that the war might have ended sooner if GIs had been able to hand out more coveted American chocolate bars to excited Europeans. In that era, the basic "Hershey bar" was a simple milk chocolate treat. As time went on and prosperity increased, once-special treats became everyday snacks, almonds were added to the Hershey bar (to start with), and snack food manufacturers recognized a good thing when they saw it.

Chocolate reportedly first came to our attention thanks to the explorer Hernando Cortez about 400 years ago, after he'd heard about it from some Aztec Indians. Milton Hershey and his heirs have managed to position the product and adapt it to changing times and changing tastes, maintaining both its appeal and its profitability.

In the 1990s, Hershey Foods Corporation was spending some $300 million a year to advertise its products. While this may not seem an excessive amount for a campaign that helped generate worldwide sales of more than $2 billion, it is in marked contrast to a 1960 article in *Sales Management*, titled "How is Hershey Doing—Without Advertising?" The answer at the time was "Very well, thank you."

Clearly, 1960 was a while ago.

In that article, a Hershey executive prophetically said, "Please make it clear that we have no quarrel with advertising. . . . The time will come when Hershey becomes an advertiser."

Hershey's chocolate is the best-selling mass-market chocolate candy bar. The brand's nod to fads might include a "cookies 'n' creme" or mint version, but its franchise was being able to put the banner reading "Made with REAL Hershey's chocolate" on a variety of food products.

Hershey products are manufactured by Hershey Chocolate U.S.A., a division of Hershey Foods Corporation. Photograph of Hershey's products by Karin Gottschalk Marconi.

Indeed. The company followed a philosophy that it has credited with building its operation to a great level of success: make a good product, sell it at the lowest possible price, and do some promotional work with retailers and distributors.

That philosophy was simple enough, but the marketing savvy the company has shown over the years demonstrates that it has kept its finger on the public pulse.

First, the Hershey chocolate brand responded to the voice of the market with a range of sizes, from the regular-size "nickel" candy bar to each extreme, with both miniature individually wrapped bite-size pieces and a large bar the physical equivalent of five regular-size candy bars.

Next, it introduced brand extensions to meet changing tastes: variations such as dark chocolate, cookies and mint in milk chocolate, and cookies 'n' creme. The gold foil–wrapped Golden Almond bar and Golden Almond Solitaires met the image requirements of baby boomers who had a need to buy everything in an upscale version, from gourmet coffee beans to candy bars.

While its corporate finger was on the pulse of the baby boomers, Hershey never forgot its other constituent groups, introducing logical derivative products, such as Hershey's toppings, Hershey's chocolate-flavored syrup, and Hershey's chocolate milk mix.

Hershey Foods is also a corporate giant that understands acquisition, diversification, and the fact that some products aren't necessarily helped by sharing the name of a famous chocolate bar. As a result, the Hershey Pasta Group is made up of a number of regional brands with names like American Beauty, Delmonico, Light 'n Fluffy, Perfection, P&R, San Giorgio, Skinner, and Ronzoni. Throughout the 1990s, most of these brands were outpacing their category in growth and showing still greater potential.

A very dramatic, yet logical, move was Hershey's extending its line of extremely popular Reese's peanut butter cups to include a crunchy version and a cookie version, as well as Reese's miniatures, Reese's peanut butter chips, Reese's peanut butter puffs breakfast cereal, Reese's peanut butter cookies, and, most logical of all, Reese's peanut butter!

Sensitive to health trends and the villainy often attributed to sweets, the company continues to pursue low-fat, low-calorie versions of its products.

As public taste moved to premium class, low-calorie, and pasta, Hershey had the financial resources and the distribution capabilities to respond aggressively. It also had

When Hershey Foods acquired the hugely popular Reese's peanut butter cups, the brand extension process began in earnest. Any competitor's product—in a candy shell, nut roll, cookie, or wafer—was fair game for a Reese's challenger. The line included Reese's peanut butter puffs breakfast cereal, peanut butter–flavored ice cream, and, as if an afterthought, jars of Reese's peanut butter.

H. B. Reese Candy Co. is a division of Hershey Foods Corporation. Photograph of Reese's products by Karin Gottschalk Marconi.

the clout, developed over more than 90 years in business under the same brand name, which it had carefully nurtured and grown.

Hershey appears to have always understood the value of its franchise. From a single fine product, it zealously guarded both the quality of the product and the integrity of the brand. It introduced extensions and acquired other brands that were a good fit with its existing products. In response to an evolving market that supported and respected the brand, it launched new products, which in turn showed Hershey's respect for its loyal distributor and customer base.

Mars, Incorporated (M&M/Mars)

M&M's bite-size chocolates in a candy shell ("The candy that melts in your mouth, not in your hand") were a longtime favorite. The brand's first brand extension, with a peanut inside, was an instant success. In the late 1980s, when food marketers launched a peanut butter explosion, M&M's were in the thick of it. Snickers, for many years America's most popular candy, introduced its own peanut butter version.

A very closely watched extension that would earn shelf space but represent a more dramatic departure from tradition was a new version of Mars's popular Milky Way candy bar, the Milky Way II, with 25 percent fewer calories than its parent. Nearly six years in development to match the flavor of the original Milky Way, the extension addressed concerns of candy-loving, health-conscious consumers. Its successor version, Milky Way Lite, expanded on the formula, emphasizing 50 percent less fat than the original Milky Way—perhaps a point-up/point-down type of benefit statement. The break with tradition was that until this time, M&M/Mars had treated its candy products as traditional sweets intended to appeal to the kid in everyone. A very popular product such as Milky Way, which had been enjoyed by kids for generations, was now being introduced in a lower-calorie version—more of an *adult* candy bar and, in that respect, opening up a new category.

In *The Sweet Truth About Confectionery*, a pamphlet published by the National Confectioners Association, the industry group attacked what it described as "myths" that have created misunderstanding among consumers. "Candy can complement your healthy and active lifestyle," an industry spokesman told the *Wall Street Journal*.

M&M's chocolate in a candy shell didn't change. The brand was successfully extended to appeal to a variety of tastes with peanuts, almonds, peanut butter, and extra crunch. Meanwhile the same company's popular Snickers and Milky Way candy bars tried to make the leap to ice cream flavors, but they were never more than a chilly novelty.

M&M's and Mars candy products are distributed by M&M/Mars, Division of Mars, Inc. Photograph of Mars products by Karin Gottschalk Marconi.

A candy industry analyst admitted, "You'd really prefer to eat the Milky Way II because of the lower calorie count and other nutritional benefits. The hard part, if you're a true confection fanatic, is the real Milky Way is notoriously better." Obviously this is an issue of great concern to nutritionists who have railed against sweets for generations.

Yet the industry takes the position that it is best to give the public what it wants, and the public has quite clearly made its feelings known. A survey by *Candy Marketer Magazine* showed that 87 percent of participating store buyers expected sales of sugar-free products to increase. The same survey said nearly half of the stores that carry sugar-free candy indicated there was a need to have more sugar-free candy on the market.

The bold move by Mars into the extension area with a modified Milky Way, multi-flavored Snickers and M&M's, and an assortment of candy bar–flavored ice cream products is in itself notable for a company that is regarded as very conservative.

Like Hershey, Mars has the resources to be bold. Annual sales for the candy division alone have topped $1.5 billion, and candy is one area where a brand can gain consumers' favor by promoting variety. If the public had rejected peanut butter–flavored Snickers, it is unlikely that the core brand Snickers candy bar would have suffered. Some years earlier the company had offered a candy bar called Forever Yours, which it positioned as, basically, a dark chocolate version of Milky Way. It never achieved significant sales and was quietly left to disappear.

In some respects, this might suggest a certain lack of forethought. First, candy marketers know that there is a significantly smaller market for dark chocolate than for milk chocolate. Note that the name Milky Way implies a milk chocolate candy. Second, Forever Yours was not a name that consciously or unconsciously had much appeal to male candy lovers; hence, the bar appealed to an older, largely female market. Finally, the brand never received a fraction of the advertising and marketing support given to Milky Way or Snickers bars.

In 1992 Mars introduced a dark chocolate Milky Way—a Forever Yours bar in a new wrapper. In the same year, Hershey brought out its Hershey's Special Dark chocolate bar. While the latter company had long included a dark chocolate candy offering in its variety pack of miniature bars, this was the first time the flavor had come into its own on the counter, both as a niche appeal product and as an extension positioned against a dark chocolate Milky Way. These two companies have the distribution machinery, promotional budgets, and retailer clout to match each other product for product, flavor for flavor, and extension for extension. It may not be war exactly, but it is competition at its most aggressive. Even in the worst of economic times, people still buy candy in all flavors and sizes, to the tune of billions of dollars per year.

Do candy makers attempt to apply their marketing savvy by reflecting the mood of the marketplace with such touches as the Big Bar and the Gold Bar (the sugar-free alternative snack bar) and even timely and trendy tributes such as the ill-fated Reggie bar (for baseball hero Reggie Jackson)? Absolutely.

In the case of Reggie, few people ever really expected it to achieve the status of its baseball predecessor candy bar Baby Ruth, which folklore has it was created to honor "The Babe." But Hershey expects to sell a lot of its Special Dark chocolate, in no small part because it has dubbed it "special," recognizing that the term "special blend" has helped sales of products from rice to cat food. (Under the Mars corporate flag have been such successful brands as Uncle Ben's rice, Kal Kan pet foods, Whiskas cat food, Sheba cat food, and Pedigree dog food.)

Companies with the resources of Mars and Hershey Foods can afford to take some risks, but smaller or more conservative companies will want to treat new entries or reentries into the crowded marketplace with care, mindful of the importance of starting with current market research.

When creating a brand extension, it is important to determine first what the public wants in terms of size, shape, or flavor, if indeed the public wants the product at all. If a marketer is sufficiently convinced that a product is so good (or even just better than its competition) and that the public will find it irresistible, test it. While research is essential to a successful launch and positioning of any product, it is especially valuable in the food product category. Few categories are as subjective when it comes to consumer tastes.

A really good marketer might be able to induce the public to come back for another try with a promise that "this year's model is faster than last year's model" or that the product "now gets your clothes even whiter," but people will long remember, and will tell their friends, about a product that doesn't taste good.

Positioning a brand correctly, according to what the public wants, is certainly part of the smoothest, if not the shortest, route to the brand's success.

Test it. Research will save costly missteps, and it is the kind of shrewd marketing dollar allocation even the penny-wise Milton Hershey would have deemed worthy.

The threshold of the twenty-first century saw no sign of the giants of candyland letting up. Hershey brought out a line called Bites, and the introduction of M&M's Crispy, a candy-coated rice-in-chocolate product, amounted to the biggest new launch in Mars history. Unlike the Coke-Pepsi "cola wars," where one of the two insists there must be a winner and a loser, the vast assortment of sweets for every sweet tooth and every taste ensures that among the candy brands, there's always room for more.

Coke and Pepsi and the Famous Cola Wars

One reason that so much of this section is devoted to the cola wars is that in Coca-Cola and Pepsi-Cola are all the elements for the classic textbook case: fiercely aggressive competitors, solid equity in both brands with strong core products, failed brand extensions, corporate politics, and some of the most successful and memorable advertising in history.

Coke and Pepsi are forever linked in the minds of consumers and professionals in industry as the most famous competitors in America, if not in the world. More than GM and Ford, or NBC and CBS, or the Democrats and the Republicans, Coke and Pepsi have made their battle to be number one as famous as their incredibly successful brands themselves.

PepsiCo, the parent company of Pepsi-Cola Company, is consistently ranked near the top of *Advertising Age*'s list of the 100 Leading National Advertisers. In the 1990s, the company's annual ad spending was more than $900 million. The Coca-Cola Company ranked well behind, with an annual ad budget of some $375 million. The wide disparity has to do with PepsiCo operating a much more diversified company than its rival. Of the two companies' flagship brands of soft drinks, actual ad spending was close to even.

Richard D. Harvey, a Seattle-based marketing consultant, has taken both companies to task, noting growth of the brands had stalled in food stores because, "They have failed to build real equity and value into their brands, turning instead to massive price-cutting backed by enormous advertising budgets featuring little more than star-studded irrelevancies."

While marketers and the public might well debate the return on multimillion-dollar fees paid for "star-studded irrelevancies" featuring performers such as Michael Jackson, Madonna, Ray Charles, and Elton John, the phrase "failed to build real equity and value into their brands" is hardly appropriate for two of the most powerful, recognizable, and profitable brands in history. In fact, a Lander Associates' Image Power Survey of Superbrands ranked Coca-Cola number one. Pepsi ranked tenth. Of the Most Powerful Brands in the United States, Coke again placed first, Pepsi was number four.

With such power and prominence comes some controversy. For all of the muscle at the supermarket, convenience store, or soda fountain that these two companies may exert, every one of their new product tests or advertisements comes under the kind of intense scrutiny and criticism normally accorded Broadway openings and tax reform. And neither company has been above tossing a zinger at the other in a show of bravado one usually associates with schoolyard rivals.

Coca-Cola

Coca-Cola is the world's bestselling soft drink, a rare product surrounded by folklore, with origins reported to be everything from a heavy-duty narcotic to a paint remover. Its formula is a more closely guarded secret than many bank vault combinations. A reliable source suggests that the beverage was invented in 1886 by John Pemberton, a then-53-year-old Georgia druggist. When a chap named Willis Venable accidentally substituted carbonated water for Pemberton's plain water, Coca-Cola was officially born as a soda fountain drink. By 1904 it was being advertised in national magazines.

The brand-building process of what was to become one of the most famous, if not *the* most famous, brands in the world had begun.

In a speech attributed to Harrison Jones, a Coca-Cola Company vice president and director of sales in the 1920s, the company is described as relentless in its pursuit of market research. Jones exhorted his sales force, "Know thy customers. . . . Know them intimately. Know them well. Have a daily tab on them. . . . If a record of purchases is kept tabulated at all times, daily, in your office, you yourself or your sales manager has constantly at hand a record of what every customer is doing and, above all, a record of what he is not doing. It is the pulse of your business and the only way to feel the pulse of your entire business at one time. It enables you to intelligently analyze and to describe and to prescribe remedies."

Brand extensions are not new to Coca-Cola. Records dating back to the 1920s have sales representatives fanning out across their assigned territories, loaded down with trunks of advertising materials, complimentary tickets, and circulars. While attempting to sell Coca-Cola fountain syrup, they would also offer for sale Coca-Cola chewing gum, cigars, and glassware bearing the Coca-Cola trademark. The glasses outsold the chewing gum and cigars.

As the company moved along from only selling syrup to bottling and selling the actual Coca-Cola soft drink to selling bottling franchises, innovations and refinements continued, such as the handy carry-home six-bottle carton. The company was also spending more than a million dollars a year on advertising.

Coca-Cola advertising both sold the product and defended Coke against charges that it contained a dangerous amount of cocaine, alcohol, or caffeine.

Some insight into the company's idea of product positioning might be gained from this advertising, as it appeared in the July 1905 issue of the national magazine the *Delineator,* from the Coca-Cola archives:

> Coca-Cola is a Delightful, Palatable, Healthful Beverage. It Relieves Fatigue and Is Indispensable for Business and Professional Men, Students, Wheelmen and Athletes, Relieves Mental and Physical Exhaustion and Is the Favorite Drink for Ladies When Thirsty, Weary, Despondent.

Not only did the product do a lot, but so did its advertising. By 1913 Coca-Cola Company claimed to have produced 5 million lithographed signs; 200,000 cutouts for window displays; 50,000 metal signs for tacking under windows; 2 million trays for soda fountains; and numerous other items from calendars to baseball cards and pencils.

Coca-Cola was everywhere—a household word in the United States and around the world. And a household word at restaurants and concession stands (fountain sales still being an enormous percentage of Coca-Cola sales). The phrase "... and a Coke" after ordering a hamburger, hot dog, popcorn, or almost anything else was common-place. While McDonald's fast-food restaurants' well-known sign notes how many billion burgers have been sold, Coca-Cola, from as far back as 1917, has been advertising how many million people each day enjoyed a Coke. By the 1950s even small children could repeat along with the television announcer

> Fifty million times a day,
> At home, at work, or on the way,
> There's nothing like a Coca-Cola
> Nothing like a Coke.

Coca-Cola has been fortunate in having management over the years that, if not always visionary, was at least competent. The company has had its share of problems but has survived handsomely. Clearly the most influential force in Coke's history was Robert W. Woodruff. He became the company's president in 1923 and ran it almost until his death in 1985 at the age of 95. A salesman and something of a showman, Woodruff would accept changes in packaging or changes in distribution, but one thing he vowed never to change was the basic core product, Coca-Cola, which he regarded as an institution. Acknowledging that the company had unsuccessfully tried its hand at brand extension around 1900 (Coca-Cola chewing gum and Coca-Cola cigars), Woodruff insisted that no further deviance or dilution of the core product or its name would occur. So it was until his retirement in 1981. That year Diet Coke was introduced with tremendous success. Woodruff did not live to see the introduction of the product New Coke, the creation of which he most certainly would have opposed.

The Coke name carried about as much clout in the marketplace as one could hope for. Management, particularly Woodruff, had emphasized the importance of building and maintaining the value—the brand equity—in the Coke name.

But the 1980s were times of increased concern about health and fitness. It went from fad to trend, with an explosion of successful and very expensive nutrition books, exercise videos, health clubs, audiotapes—even the music and wardrobe to go with it. Sweet, syrupy cola beverages were being passed over in favor of fruit juices, teas, and bottled water until the industry caught on and began offering sugar-free cola drinks. They were rarely as satisfying or flavorful as their sugary originals, but the public still bought into the idea in a big way.

Coca-Cola's entry into the diet cola business was Tab, a reflection of Woodruff's insistence that the Coca-Cola name belonged only on Coke. Despite the small print line "a product of the Coca-Cola Company" on its packaging, Tab technically did not qualify as a brand extension, nor should it have. Tab's taste and packaging did nothing to suggest Coca-Cola. The product did fairly well, but it never drew anywhere near the interest or sales figures of the parent company's flagship product.

With the retirement of Woodruff and the subsequent dawning of a new philosophy, the Coke name became unconstrained and entered a period of great expansion and extension.

The introduction of Diet Coke was not so much a product launch as a media event, with some 6 thousand invited guests gathering at New York's Radio City Music Hall to be entertained by singer Bobby Short, the Radio City Rockettes, and a 40-piece orchestra. A 14-foot can of Diet Coke rose on cue from the orchestra pit. The event was filmed, and its highlights were incorporated into the first Diet Coke TV commercials to underscore the momentous nature of the event and the product.

Not only did Diet Coke rapidly become the third-largest-selling soft drink in the United States, but it was awarded the honor of being named "Brand of the Decade" by the editors of *Advertising Age.*

Coca-Cola's true foray into the area of modern brand extension was more than a success; it was the stuff of product-marketing history. Bolstered by this success, Coke began to sense changing public tastes in which consumers seemed to be focusing on a desire for more and greater choices. The company embarked on a serious brand extension program that by 1985 would change the way people thought of Coke. Consumers would have the opportunity to choose from a soft drink menu that included Coca-Cola, Caffeine-Free Coke, Diet Coke, Caffeine-Free Diet Coke, and Cherry Coke, as well as the company's non-cola beverages, such as Sprite (to counter 7-Up), Mr. Pibb (to challenge Dr. Pepper), flavored sodas under the Fanta label, and Tab, still hanging in but well under the shadow of Diet Coke.

Coca-Cola had succeeded in responding to changing public tastes and trends and in retaining both its dominance on supermarket shelves and its worldwide preeminence as the consumers' choice among soft drinks—*all* soft drinks.

But no review of the company's marketing strategy can overlook what will be debated for decades as either the greatest exercise in corporate misjudgment or the greatest publicity stunt of the modern age: the introduction of New Coke.

The *Wall Street Journal* announced, "New Coke Shows the Risks of Research," adding, "When the Coca-Cola Company uncorked its new formula in April 1985, executives boasted it was the surest move they had ever made. They described as 'overwhelming' the results of taste tests with 190,000 consumers, the majority of whom preferred the new recipe over the old Coke. By now, of course, everyone is well aware that it wasn't a sure thing."

Despite the often-repeated adage "If it ain't broke, don't fix it," the Coca-Cola Company announced that it would alter the taste of the world's best-selling, most popular soft drink.

The reason for this drastic move was that Coke's number-one rival, Pepsi, was gaining on Coke in market share. This new formulation was expected to appeal to Pepsi drinkers, while still being Coke to Coke drinkers.

The successful introduction of Diet Coke in Radio City Music Hall was a hard act to follow by anyone's standards, but the advance word was that the Coca-Cola Company on April 23, 1985, would offer security analysts and the press "the most important announcement in the company's 99-year history."

Thomas L. Harris, public relations consultant and associate professor of corporate public relations at Northwestern University's Medill School of Journalism, recounted, "Hundreds of reporters and analysts attending in a theater in Lincoln Center learned about the reformulation of Coca-Cola. Media headlines made the world aware of 'New Coke' overnight, touching off an immediate and negative reaction. The 'New Coke,' the now legendary product failure, reminded people how much they loved the old Coke, and put it back on top. Donald Keough, Coca-Cola's president, said that 'all the time and money and skill poured into market research on the new Coca-Cola could not measure or reveal the deep and abiding emotional attachment to Coca-Cola.'"

Keough also said, "Some cynic will say that we planned the whole thing for the publicity value. The truth is that we are not that dumb and we are not that smart."

The experience is fascinating in part because there was no apparent reason to change the product initially. Why change when you're number one? And blaming market research for such a huge negative reaction seemed a bit of a stretch on two counts: First, who, with a straight face, would have ever looked for or characterized anyone as having a "deep and abiding emotional attachment" to a soft drink? And second, researchers *are* skilled in reading emotional reactions, and it is difficult to believe that out of 190,000 tests no evidence of such an intense feeling surfaced.

Most significant is that "being smart" isn't related to just getting all the publicity. It is in being able to reintroduce your original product (perhaps for the first time in history) with a legitimate claim to the phrase "back by popular demand," and to use the word *classic* on your product with justification rather than having it look like a reformulated brand extension. "Classic," it is safe to suggest, is a much more powerful term than "original formula."

Many marketers believed that the Coca-Cola Company should have let the matter drop while it was ahead. It still had New Coke on the market to appeal to Pepsi lovers, and now it had Coke Classic.

Coke Classic racked up great sales and, while the figures weren't spectacular, the company *did* sell a fair amount of New Coke. Imagine the surprise of those true believers who seriously thought that the company had simply made a mistake, when Coca-Cola announced in March 1990 that it planned to reintroduce New Coke under the name Coke II with new packaging.

Apparently pleased with the two-year test run in Spokane, Washington, the company plugged Coke II into Chicago outlets with a huge TV ad campaign, including a competitive ad taking aim at Pepsi. With not much of an attempt at subtlety, the ad copy read: "Real cola taste, plus the sweetness of Pepsi."

How effective was this frontal assault on the competition?

Fewer than a quarter of the people who saw the test commercial could repeat it. The trouble might have involved overlooking one of the basic elements of good, effective advertising. Where was the USP (unique selling proposition)? The ad test appraisal was that "Coke II may have a problem in that what's being communicated—a new name—isn't persuading soft drink purchasers to buy the product."

Consumers may *try* a product because of its name, but it's a pretty big leap of faith to assume that, after having rejected it, they will try it again just because the company repositioned it and changed the product's name.

How is it that a company so savvy, so obsessed with collecting research data in its early years, was now trying to blame research for a product failure? Here was a smart marketer with a lot of research and testing, apparently failing to learn what a market test so easily concluded: that its ad for a new product was not all that persuasive.

Whether it is called New Coke or Coke II, this product clearly stands to be a continuing embarrassment to the Coca-Cola Company. A cardinal rule in brand-extension strategy is that the potential for negative reflection on the core brand must be eliminated or held to a minimum. Obviously a product called Coke II can hardly distance or disassociate itself from its core brand, Coke. It *can* take a niche marketing approach and focus on certain of its characteristics, such as a sweetness that's not for every taste. So if the brand extension fizzles out, it might be dismissed on the basis of its niche characteristics, rather than leaving a residue that could stain the core product.

Taking on Pepsi with a guns-blazing, confrontational campaign is bold. It might have worked if it carried a benefit (tastes better, lower cost, fewer calories, larger size), but an attack without a clear reason to win is an ill-conceived notion.

Sales of Coke Classic have held their own and sales of Diet Coke have risen. Coke II, even after quietly disappearing from store shelves and vending machines for lack of interest, will unfortunately be remembered as proof that not everything with the Coke name on it will be accepted as the *real thing*, or a sure thing, even by the most loyal consumers.

In January 1993, Coca-Cola again went head-to-head with Pepsi on a brand extension, although this time the company seemed to be trying to learn from its past mistakes. When Pepsi-Cola, responding to growing public interest in things pure (or at least things that *looked* pure), launched a new clear beverage called Crystal Pepsi (and an extension of the extension, Diet Crystal Pepsi), Coca-Cola responded with Tab Clear.

While Pepsi-Cola told the industry that it believed the "clear cola" provided a positive complement to their existing products and "broadens the appeal of our trademark," Coco-Cola held back, unwittingly undercutting its Tab product by vehemently insisting there would never be a clear Coke. Further, while both Coke and Pepsi have mainstream appeal, Tab has long carried the image of being the beverage of choice of women dieters.

Within a year, the "clear" craze appeared to have run its course. Crystal Pepsi, Diet Crystal Pepsi, and Tab Clear went on to join New Coke and Coke II in soft drink heaven.

In their continuing cola wars, the makers of Coke and Pepsi appear to recognize that in times of instant international news dissemination and broad interest in winners and losers, what is at stake is more than a cola. An evening television news story announcing that one competing product has hit the dust can mean sales success and image enhancement for the winner and can determine the price and direction of the company's stock. Coca-Cola cannot afford too many perceived misjudgments or ill-positioned product launches. Its stockholders will react in the same way as those of any other large corporation would, exhorting management to "get it right or get lost."

The Coca-Cola experience in brand building and brand extension may be the example of the best and the worst. The "most powerful brand in the world," with a franchise recognized from Atlanta to Albania, is obviously doing something right—and has been for more than a hundred years. Yet a single brand extension failure has left a deep gash in the company's shining armor. Coca-Cola gum and Coca-Cola cigars could just be dropped and forgotten. However, the huge amount of publicity attending a modern brand-extension launch, with its large-budget, mass communication blitz, is a double-edged sword. First impressions, public perceptions, and early reviews can stamp something a success or a failure instantly, with headlines that drive the message home. Once a stumble is

caught in the mass media, the picture painted is very difficult to erase.

For all its might, power, and successful launches to
date, Coke will be under increasingly greater scrutiny as
the competitive field becomes more crowded and the
stakes get even higher.

Pepsi-Cola

One reason Coke will be under greater pressure is that
Pepsi will demand it. Pepsi-Cola has proved to be Coca-
Cola's only serious rival over the years, though many have
tried. Pepsi-Cola has even, on occasion, gone as far as to
claim victory in the cola war. Indeed, a book coauthired
by Pepsi's then-CEO Roger Enrico was titled *The Other Guy
Blinked: How Pepsi Won the Cola Wars.*

Alas, the victory celebration may have been a bit
premature.

Like Coca-Cola, Pepsi-Cola was the creation of a South-
ern druggist, Caleb Bradham of North Carolina. Offering
various combinations and soft drink mixtures at his drug-
store soda fountain, Bradham developed a drink that people called "Brad's drink" in his honor in the 1890s. By
1898 Bradham had named it Pepsi-Cola, in part because he
believed the drink could effectively settle an upset stom-
ach (dyspepsia) and relieve the pain of peptic ulcers. The
popularity of the drink grew steadily, and the Pepsi-Cola
Company was formed in 1902. By 1910 the company's
operations had grown to include a network of 280 bottlers
in 24 states.

While Pepsi-Cola was tremendously successful, by 1920
fluctuations in sugar prices following World War I forced a
financial reversal and a change in ownership, effectively
forcing an end to Bradham's career as a soft drink tycoon.

Reorganized and under new management, the company moved to Virginia. Its new owner lacked the marketing ability necessary to make the operation a success, and

with an added shove from the Great Depression, by 1931 Pepsi was bankrupt for the second time.

Destined to become the phoenix of the soft drink world, Pepsi was bought by Charles Guth, president of Loft Stores, a chain of candy stores that dispensed an annual volume of Coca-Cola that amounted to about 1 percent of the beverage company's total sales. Guth believed that if he could switch from Coke to Pepsi without customer complaints, he could significantly increase his profits.

The Pepsi-Cola Company at that time represented little more than a formula, so Guth assigned Richard Ritchie, a chemist employed in his candy laboratory, to help improve the situation. Over the two years that followed, Loft Stores bought about half the Pepsi syrup sold. What was hoped would be profitable was operating at a loss. Coke was well known; Pepsi was not. When the Loft Stores changed beverages, sales plummeted.

Convinced that the venture had been a complete failure, in 1933 Guth attempted to sell Pepsi-Cola to Coca-Cola. It was a later decision, however, that amounted to a major reversal of fortune for Pepsi. That decision was to sell 12-ounce bottles of Pepsi to wholesalers in such a way that retailers could offer them at the same price as standard 6.5-ounce bottles. The benefit to the customer was that the same price bought twice as much Pepsi as it did Coke. After a sputtering start, the process was refined and by 1934 was declared a success. Pepsi once again looked to be on its way.

Corporate politics being the way of the world, after considerable legal wrangling with Loft, Guth was forced to surrender his Pepsi-Cola stock, but not before he had set the company on a profitable course. His belief was that the strength, popularity, and brand loyalty of Coca-Cola was so great that the only way Pepsi-Cola could make a difference was in its price. He was proved right. While Coca-Cola continued to maintain its hold as the clear leader in its industry, well-capitalized and profitable even during the Depression, Pepsi-Cola was still that ambitious upstart company that wouldn't go away.

While the business community at large may not have viewed Pepsi as a threat to Coke, the Coca-Cola Company was taking no chances. The David and Goliath of the soft drink industry, on occasion, even found themselves facing off in court . . . and not always over the predictable infringement issue.

Despite Guth being ousted as head of Pepsi-Cola, his former employer, Loft Stores, still held his stock and continued serving Pepsi in its stores. When detectives working undercover for Coca-Cola found Loft customers who ordered Coke were being served Pepsi without their knowledge, Coca-Cola sued, charging "substitution." Coca-Cola did not win its case but went back to court, next charging Pepsi-Cola with trademark infringement. A variety of stories have circulated about exactly what happened during that period, but the end result was a quiet out-of-court settlement that dropped Coca-Cola's lawsuit and kept Pepsi-Cola going. The time was 1942.

With these early battles in the cola wars, nothing was happening to seriously threaten Coke's dominance. However, Coca-Cola still bristled over the package size issue. Coca-Cola bottlers had an enormous investment in equipment and materials, hence the reluctance to change from their standard 6.5-ounce bottles. Since 1929 the company and its bottlers had suffered through hearing the jingle

> Pepsi-Cola hits the spot
> Twelve full ounces, that's a lot
> Twice as much for a nickel, too
> Pepsi-Cola is the drink for you.

This classic advertising jingle, like other classics, almost never saw light. Guth's successor as head of Pepsi-Cola, the entrepreneurial securities dealer Walter Mack, wanted to run the jingle as a radio commercial without the usual

...ouncer's pitch. This was unheard of at the time. Both Pepsi-Cola's advertising agency and CBS radio insisted that the audience wouldn't get the point of a stand-alone jingle without a sales message. Mack's response was to take his message elsewhere, to radio stations that needed the business and were willing to allow him to do what he wanted, when he wanted, and how he wanted. The result was that Pepsi-Cola sales soared wherever the jingle played. CBS and the ad agency relented. Some claim that this incident represented the birth of the 30-second radio spot, subsequently the norm in radio and television advertising.

Coca-Cola for years had relied on its slogan "the pause that refreshes," which by all accounts had become an effective and recognizable tag. When Pepsi-Cola again tried to push its more-for-your-money theme with a new slogan of its own, "more bounce to the ounce," critics were divided as to its effectiveness.

Author and former publicist Michael Gershman thought the catchy new line "gave Pepsi an image boost and it became second only to Coca-Cola in soft drink sales. Pepsi sales soared and for the first time Coca-Cola sales slumped."

Yet Harvard professor Richard S. Tedlow wrote, "At the end of the 1940s, Pepsi launched yet another slogan—*more bounce to the ounce.* This slogan was designed to claim that Pepsi-Cola was not only more in volume, but in qualitative terms as well, that it had more punch and provided more energy than its competitor. The slogan commanded no credibility among consumers."

Regardless of which version one chooses to accept, Coca-Cola finally conceded the competitive realities of the packaging issue and that its product was more costly when compared with Pepsi. Coke introduced "king size" and "family size" bottles in 1955. For taking so long to bring out its own 12-ounce bottle, Coca-Cola, the industry leader, had to endure charges that it was copying Pepsi-Cola.

Higher production costs forced Pepsi-Cola to raise its price, thus softening its claim of being the better value for the money. Pepsi-Cola's market share declined as Coke's rose. Pepsi-Cola's response once again was to hope that new leadership with new ideas would strengthen its competitive position. That new leadership arrived in the person of Alfred Steele, a former Coca-Cola vice president who was hired by Walter Mack. (Mack, although being named chairman of the board in order to make room for Steele as president, felt he had been treated badly and left Pepsi-Cola shortly after the changing of the guard.)

The new leadership that Steele provided included some 15 management people he had brought over with him from the Coca-Cola Company. Some might claim that this dramatic turning point for Pepsi, allowing it to somewhat narrow the gap, came by way of hiring away so much of the rival's key talent.

Among Steele's contributions were improving relationships with bottlers and "standardizing" Pepsi's taste, as tested in bottling plants across the country; investing heavily in new equipment; and reducing the product's sugar content, thereby creating a lighter-tasting drink with fewer calories.

A major part of the new Pepsi strategy was to focus on age. Coke had been around awhile, and it was familiar. Pepsi-Cola tried to make it look *old*. The "Pepsi Generation" ad campaign proved to be both brilliant and enduring, a position statement of enormous impact./In its brand-building efforts, Pepsi had evolved from "Pepsi-Cola hits the spot" to "more bounce to the ounce" to "the Pepsi Generation—for those who think young."

While the "Pepsi Generation" campaign was heavy on imagery and light on product benefits, its newest publicity stunt launched one of the most successful and long-running promotional gambits in modern marketing: "The Pepsi Challenge," introduced in Dallas, Texas, in 1974.

Pepsi-Cola insisted that its product was preferred overwhelmingly in blind taste tests with Coke. Soon the challenge was expanded to other markets and, in a very gutsy move, was even incorporated into live commercials on national television.

In his book *The Other Guy Blinked: How Pepsi Won the Cola Wars,* Enrico writes, "Pepsi enjoyed 72 straight months of market share growth. By 1974, the Pepsi-Cola brand had pulled even with Coke in food stores. In 1977, Pepsi pulled ahead—permanently."

Well . . . maybe not. Claiming that Pepsi has won the cola wars is like asking a bully who is pummeling you if he gives up. Pepsi has done well—certainly better than anyone else—as a Coke competitor. But in terms of soft drink sales, more than 10 years after Enrico made that statement, Pepsi, alas, still had not *won*. Sales of Coke still dominated, both domestically and around the world.

With nothing quite approaching the unfortunate experience of New Coke, Pepsi, too, has had its less-than-shining moments.

One of them was Pepsi Free.

In his book Enrico described it as "among the most successful new brands in the history of American consumer products." This caffeine-free cola *did* roll out strong before sales collapsed and the brand totally faded from sight. A caffeine-free cola with a touch of lemon flavoring was an interesting enough idea to try, but not interesting enough to become the beverage of choice for enough people to keep it alive.

At the other end of the spectrum was the caffeine-*heavy* Pepsi A.M., a new product that faded so quickly that Enrico didn't even mention it in his book. Pepsi A.M. was introduced as a drink for people who wanted an alternative to that morning cup of coffee. Market research indicated that in most regions of the United States, cola drinking starts around lunchtime and continues through the end of the day. But in some warm climates, cola was as welcome a morning drink as coffee or tea. Market researchers neglected to ascertain whether consumers felt that to enjoy a cola drink in the morning, it needed to have the letters

"A.M." in its name. People didn't grasp why they needed to buy one Pepsi for mornings and another for the rest of the day.

A can of Pepsi A.M. is now regarded as a collector's item.

Diet Pepsi, on the other hand, was a smashing success.

While Diet Coke has remained consistently ahead, sales figures for Diet Pepsi have been excellent from the start.

Pepsi-Cola was counting on big things for its Crystal Pepsi clear color, regular and diet, but both products "went flat."

Continuing in an aggressive mode, in 1993 Pepsi-Cola launched Pepsi Max, a sugar-free cola with a sweetener that the FDA (U.S. Food and Drug Administration) was slow to approve but the rest of the world allowed. The company insisted that the sweetener produced the closest match to the original taste. Alas, Americans will never know if that statement was true or just a kind of Pepsi Free/Pepsi A.M. hype.

While Enrico relishes recounting Coca-Cola's embarrassment over New Coke (hence his claim of Pepsi's victory), he adds in a more sober tone, "By now both of us know that neither Pepsi nor Coke wins decisively in this game. There will always be other battles on other fronts keeping us too busy to celebrate. And if we fail . . . well, we've both failed before and picked ourselves up off the floor."

An advertising trade magazine once asked, "What's the big idea worth?" Will future students of advertising and marketing recognize the genius of Coca-Cola's "the pause that refreshes" or "It's the Real Thing," and forgive Pepsi-Cola for such disasters as "You've got the right one, baby—uh-huh," while saluting "The choice of a new generation"?

Very likely, yes.

The search for the right words to define or position a brand is compared by some marketers to the search for the Holy Grail. Pepsi-Cola has certainly won some and lost some, and it will continue to do so.

Some of Pepsi's More Memorable Slogans

- Pepsi-Cola hits the spot
- More bounce to the ounce
- Twice as much for a penny more
- Say "Pepsi, please"
- Be sociable, look smart
- Come alive—you're in the Pepsi generation
- For those who think young
- The Pepsi Challenge, Taste that beats the others cold
- You've got a lot to live . . .
  and Pepsi's got a lot to give
- The choice of a new generation
- You've got the right one, baby—uh-huh

In 1998, without fanfare, the brand introduced a one-calorie line extension called PepsiOne. Perhaps it had learned from New Coke that raising expectations could be risky, but the lack of an aggressive marketing campaign could also suggest a lack of confidence in the extension of the brand.

Dixie Cup

What matters most is what's on the inside, the expression goes. According to history, sometimes maybe not.

Over the years, many an exasperated parent has looked on as a child beams with joy upon receiving a wonderful, special gift . . . and then spends the day playing with the box it came in. Try to imagine such a situation in the world of brand marketing.

Dixie Cup's story comes pretty close.

By the 1990s, Dixie Cup had become virtually the

generic name for paper cups. The brand's origin, however, begins with a statement of noble purpose of which few consumers may be aware.

Hugh Moore had an idea that seemed so obvious, he was sure its time had come. Early in the twentieth century, folks commonly quenched their thirst by drawing a tin dipper of water from a barrel outside a store, railway station, or wherever. Moore looked on incredulously as people came and went, drinking from the same dipper, which was never washed or replaced. He realized that all sorts of waterborne diseases were thriving and multiplying. In this public health spirit, Moore saw a money-making opportunity. He convinced an investment banker that any number of communicable diseases might be alleviated by replacing the dippers with individual cups, and the banker helped arrange a meeting with American Can Company's president, William Graham. It was Graham who provided the initial $200,000 to finance Hugh Moore's venture. Thus, the Public Cup Vendor Company was born in 1908 in New York City.

First, the company began producing porcelain vending machines that, for a penny, sold a five-ounce cup of clean, cold spring water.

While most New Yorkers saw no benefit in paying for something that was so readily available free, medical professionals applauded both the machine and its reason for existing. Because of this, health professionals became prime prospects to buy the machine, and they did.

As additional needs for clean, sanitary cups became more apparent, Moore recognized that distributing and selling the *cups* in his vending machine made a lot more sense than trying to sell water. He said, "We had to sell the idea that drinking water out of dirty glasses was dangerous."

Despite the numerous medical reports and studies available in 1908, the idea that water carried germs, and germs meant disease, was still treated in a cavalier manner by consumers. With growing support from public health officials and medical practitioners, Moore was able to secure business from a number of railway companies and other businesses. The public at large still treated the sharing of public dippers and drinking cups with indifference.

Moore's Public Cup Vendor Company became the Individual Drinking Cup Company and, later, Health Kup, but as much as he believed in his product and its value, its worth was largely unrecognized. Cups and drinking glasses were items people took for granted. The challenge was to establish the product's value and then identify that value with the brand. Searching for an upbeat, less clinical-sounding name than Health Kup, he noticed the name on the door of a neighboring office, the Dixie Doll Company, and from this inspiration Dixie Cup was born.

Even with its catchy new name, the company continued to struggle for another four years, until its owner saw an opportunity. Prior to the 1940s, ice cream was sold only in bulk and ice cream makers were struggling, with business in a flat period. Many feared that the simple candy bar would become a formidable sweet shop competitor. Moore and ice cream makers believed they had found a way to do each other some good. The machinery and technology of the Dixie Cup company was employed to pack ice cream into two-and-a-half-ounce paper cups. The plan worked.

Gershman said of the Dixie Cup story in his appropriately titled book *Getting It Right the Second Time*, "Hugh Moore and his partner Lawrence Luellen . . . were thrilled to be selling their cups in quantity to somebody, anybody." What neither of them foresaw was that by packaging ice cream in a neat, convenient container, they were also popularizing small, disposable paper cups. Just as institutions later familiarized masses of people with frozen foods, consumers subconsciously began to accept the idea of a paper cup as a disposable container for solids, semisolids, and liquids.

For the first time in marketing history, a package became synonymous with the product it contained. As if it were generic, the name for any kind of ice cream in any kind of handy little cup became known as a *Dixie Cup*.

As the public became more and more accustomed to the concept of the disposable paper cup, the added benefits of how convenient and sanitary it was became easy to embrace.

In the minds of many people, Dixie Cup was first and foremost in the disposable cup business. The ice cream product became an extension of the brand. Others will contend that it was the other way around—that Dixie Cup really failed to make its mark until it went into the ice cream business, thus making the individual disposable cup an extension of that product. In any case, Moore's idea of a safer, more sanitary product may not have taken the route he had originally intended, but it ended up at the correct destination.

In marketing terms, Dixie Cup was an example of a product hitchhiking or piggybacking another product to succeed. In this case it was piggybacking paper cups on ice cream. It could also be termed a turnaround success, a product being adapted successfully for a purpose for which it had not originally been intended and finding a new and larger market. It is ironic that Dixie Cup has come full circle, far less identified with ice cream and more commonly thought of as an individual, sanitary, disposable drinking cup.

By the 1990s, the company was claiming that some 42 million Dixie Cups, in various sizes and colors, hot and cold versions, were used each day. The name Dixie Cup, whether on an ice cream cup or an empty cup, was associated with a quality in the minds of consumers. The name had come to symbolize the brand more than the product, and the product served to enhance the name.

Xerox: A Humbling Experience Made a Good Brand Better

Xerox achieved the kind of unique status as a brand that most brand managers dream about . . . and the company's lawyers want everyone to know that they are none too happy about it.

The preeminent copy machine manufacturer in the United States had built both the product and the market for it. As a result, the Xerox name has been applied incorrectly to the products of countless competitors. According to the company's lawyers, it's OK to ask for a copy, a photocopy, or a photostat of a document, but if you ask for "a Xerox" or "a Xerox copy," the brand of the machine used to produce it had better be Xerox or you may be opening yourself up to possible legal action.

Xerox is a registered trademark of the Xerox Corporation, but the word, like *Coke* and *Kleenex*, is used as the generic name for the product, not as the name of a specific brand. Certainly Xerox believes it dilutes the value of the brand name if people think that they are getting Xerox copies from machines manufactured by Canon, Kodak, Sharp, Minolta, or any of numerous others.

Adding insult to injury, the company that built the market had to endure the humiliation of being outsold by "cheap imitators," many of which were very good.

According to *Fortune* magazine, "Even though the company brought out the first copiers in 1949, it was being clobbered in the 1980s by Japanese rivals selling machines at the same price that it cost Xerox to make them. Xerox's biggest corporate sin: arrogantly taking customers for granted. The company wasn't too effective with employees either."

"I frankly thought Xerox was on its way out of business," recalls former Xerox CEO David Kearns.

At an earlier time, Japanese-made products had been dismissed as cheap and inferior by consumers in the

United States and other countries. Brands such as Sony, Toyota, Yamaha, and Nissan changed that. Modern Japanese technology and competitiveness, especially in the electronics and automotive industries, frequently produced products that set new standards for quality.

The entry of Japanese companies into the copier business was no less impressive.

To keep matters in order and in perspective, it must be acknowledged that Xerox was an absolutely first-class company. Its history is the stuff of which folklore is made. In the 1930s, Chester Carlson, living in a cramped one-room apartment, working in a makeshift laboratory in Astoria, Queens, New York, invented a process called xerography—document copying without printing or tracing. He tried to sell this process to every important company in the office equipment business, including IBM, General Electric, RCA, Remington Rand, and about 20 others. They all passed. Finally, a relatively small operation in Rochester, New York, The Haloid Company, showed an interest in Carlson and his process. After a shaky start, in its crudest form, the process that would revolutionize print communications was under way.

In 1955 Chester Carlson signed over full title to all of his patents in exchange for 50,000 shares of Haloid stock. The process was generating enough interest that the company had changed its name to Haloid Xerox. By 1961 it had evolved into the Xerox Corporation.

The company, despite numerous fits and starts, grew rapidly. On occasion, the company would delay the introduction of its new models for fear of smothering sales of existing models that were still doing well. The "Xerox machine" was the essential piece of office equipment after the telephone. It made even the smallest company look big.

Building the brand was not difficult, as the machine was useful, visible, and virtually without competition.

By the 1960s, Xerox profits were high, sales were great, and the company had indeed achieved the status of becom-

When the dream becomes a nightmare . . . Few brands are both lucky and unlucky enough to meet the fate of Kleenex, Coke, and Xerox. These brands are so successful as to be treated generically by much of the marketplace—a place where any cola is a Coke and any photocopy a Xerox. The success can cost the brands untold millions when substitutes are offered and/or accepted without hesitation.

Kleenex is a registered trademark for a line of products from Kimberly-Clark Corporation.

ing a household word. Yet some people wondered what would happen to Xerox if someone else came out with a cheaper or faster product than the now fully perfected process of xerography.

It is ironic that Chester Carlson had taken his early idea to the office equipment and computer giant IBM and had been turned away. In later years, talks were initiated more than once between the two companies for the purpose of selling patents or entering into joint ventures, but nothing ever came of them. By 1970 IBM wanted in, but its position in the market, at least for the copy machine segment, was to be an afterthought. As Al Ries and Jack Trout note in their book *Positioning*, "IBM is a much bigger company than Xerox and has awesome resources of technology, workforce, and money. Yet what happened when IBM introduced a line of copiers competitive with those of Xerox? Not much. Xerox still has a share of the copier market several times that of IBM."

The first one to succeed in a given industry or category and become the market leader has the advantage of being so identified as to "own" that market. Even a powerful and formidable competitor like IBM could not shake from people's minds that a copy machine was a *Xerox* machine.

Xerox had built a brand with so much perceived equity, it could beat back the strongest potential competition. Then, in the parlance of the business community, the wheel fell off.

Two factors kicked in, either of which might have been enough to demolish the company. One problem was external, the other internal. In the 1992 book *Prophets in the Dark*, former Xerox CEO David Kearns described the internal situation, noting that "Given the environment [of our success] it was easy for managers to get a little arrogant and stop paying attention to what the competition we did have was doing and to drift out of intimate contact with the customer. We got into big trouble mostly because we stopped listening to the customer. Sooner or later that sort of deafness can be fatal."

Kearns continued, "There was also no real quality control to speak of in the company, no all-pervasive attitude that the products must be as good as humanly possible. Quality in those days was considered nothing more than an expense—and who wanted extra expenses?"

Kearns points out that even Xerox pricing policies were alienating the company's customers, and one could hardly blame them for being upset. Their pricing was "about the most bewildering strategy I ever came across; you'd get dizzy looking at all the presentations."

At the same time, the external situation grew more threatening. While managers at Xerox had expected that at some point Japanese companies would enter their business, no one paid much attention to the threat. Presumably the sentiment was that if Xerox was strong enough and smart enough to best the likes of giants such as IBM and Kodak, it could certainly withstand the challenges of foreign competitors. Further, no one seemed to take note of two characteristics of well-run, successful Japanese companies: they offered a high level of quality for products manufactured at a very low cost.

Savin, in a joint venture with Japanese manufacturer Ricoh, offered a copier that broke down less often, was easier to repair, and was priced at less than half the cost of a comparable Xerox machine. Obviously, it was a huge success.

And that was only the beginning.

Other Japanese companies kept the pressure on and chipped away at the Xerox market share. Much of the chipping seemed to come in very large chunks, as the perception became reality. While Xerox was still the original and the U.S. leader in the field of copiers, there were fine, even superior, machines available at a lower cost.

At the same time, a Xerox attempt at diversification into non-copier fields was not going well. IBM tried its hand at getting into Xerox's business and stumbled. In an ironic turn, Xerox's foray into the computer-based information systems business was a similar failure.

Xerox had purchased a company called Scientific Data Systems and, treating it as a brand extension of the copier line rather than a mere subsidiary, changed its name to Xerox Data Systems. The billion-dollar acquisition depended heavily on government contracts, particularly for the U.S. space program, for its survival. The acquisition occurred, coincidentally, at a time when such contracts were drying up, causing the venture to be a money-loser from day one. With Xerox's stock price falling, the company tried a number of reconfigurations of Xerox Data Systems, separating operating units and separating functions. After six years and enormous losses, Xerox folded Xerox Data Systems.

Undeterred, the company pursued other ventures, such as moving into the personal computer arena, seeing it quite correctly as a huge emerging growth area. Alas, it was not to be Xerox's fate to profit from this new emergence. In the minds of the overwhelming majority of people, Xerox remained still a copier company, and one that was being badly beaten up by the Japanese.

A major reason for this, again, was said to be Xerox's failure to listen to its customers, to take the pulse of its markets. Virtually all Xerox copy machines were leased to customers, who bought supplies and maintenance services from the company. By the 1970s, this scenario changed as Xerox's competition had made ownership of copy machines very affordable. Leases were not renewed. Contracts were cancelled.

Kearns examined the totality of the situation and announced, "The deeper we studied what was going on in our industry, the worse things looked."

The only possible way out of this quagmire, the company concluded, lay in two options: either diversifying or almost completely changing the way the company did business, from manufacturing and quality control to pricing and marketing. Amid much debate, the company chose to do both.

Diversification took the form of acquiring companies that were (1) more tied to the service industry than to manufacturing and (2) industries where the type of problems that Xerox had experienced in the past were unlikely to occur. To put it more bluntly, that meant looking for companies to acquire in which competitors, such as Japanese industrialists, would not move in and produce a better product at a lower cost.

Starting in 1992 with the purchase of the very prosperous casualty insurance operation Crum & Forster, Xerox financial Services was born. Two profitable investment banking businesses were acquired: Van Kampen Merritt and Furman Selz. Xerox Life and Xerox credit were added to the roster and a stake in VMS Realty Partners rounded out the mix.

Through most of the 1980s, Xerox financial Services seemed to be exactly the right prescription to offset the losses on the parent company's office products side and to contribute mightily to the bottom line. In some periods, a larger percentage of income was generated from the financial services operation than from the original core products. The company had acquired profitable companies that had products the public wanted. Whether or not a copier company's name added credibility to mutual funds was a subject for debate. What *was* clear, however, was that customers felt better buying—and brokers felt better selling—products with a name the public already knew, even if it was not a name readily associated with the products being offered.

Ultimately, a rough economy, radical changes in laws affecting the insurance industry, and tax law changes that almost wiped away real estate syndication left at least a couple of Xerox financial Services units to crash and burn.

The major change, important to both its revolutionary makeover of Xerox and its long-term importance, was the manufacturing, pricing, and marketing process. The emphasis was on quality and, in a marked departure from the company's past, on listening to customers. Kearns described his years with Xerox as the "blooming of quality." They had corporate problem solvers organize problem areas into six principles on which their "intensification efforts for quality" would be based:

1. A customer defines our business.

2. Our success depends upon the involvement and empowerment of trained and highly motivated people.

3. Line management must lead quality improvement.

4. Management develops, articulates, and deploys clear direction and objectives.

5. Quality challenges are met and satisfied.

6. The business is managed and improved by using facts.

Product quality improved. Reliability improved. Customer satisfaction increased. Labor overhead was trimmed by 50 percent, materials overhead was cut by 40 percent, and the process of relationship building went into high gear.

Xerox's efforts had not only stopped its slide, they reversed the company's course and rocketed the Xerox product and brand back to respectability. It was again a leading worldwide manufacturer and a good name. In 1982 Xerox did not have a single machine rated best in its class by industry analysts, but by 1992, Xerox models were ranked the leading machines in all seven copier categories.

Most significant was that Xerox was the first major company targeted by Japanese manufacturers to turn the tide and take back the market solely by its own efforts. There was no government assistance, no bailout, and no legislation or merger with another company.

Xerox came back, but without question it did it the hard way. Perhaps the key point that saved the company was a willingness by its management to take a hard, critical, and honest look at itself and then create a plan to take corrective measures. Corporate arrogance had hurt it badly, and that had to be changed. The company needed to listen to its customers and be responsive. It needed to put the emphasis on producing quality products at competitive prices. It wasn't enough anymore just to be Xerox.

It needed also to look at those acquisitions and divisions to which it had attached its brand name. The failure of Scientific Data Systems was all the more damaging because it was called Xerox Data Systems at the time of its liquidation. The ultimate collapse of Crum & Forster would have had far worse implications for the brand had it been called Xerox Property and Casualty Company. Bad enough that it was a featured part of the highly advertised Xerox financial Services. Diversification, brand extensions, and acquisitions are certainly legitimate options for a company—quite often part of a great and creative strategy. But the options have to make sense financially as well as enhance the core brand or company image. They cannot expose the company or the brand to an unknown degree of potential damage if the extension or acquisition fails.

Obviously, there are no "sure things," as great companies such as Coca-Cola and Pepsi-Cola found out. But to follow a quick-fix course of action in a moment of desperation must be considered at best a very high-risk strategy.

Xerox clearly had done some things very right and some very wrong. Even the company's top brass conceded that for a long time survival, much less profitability, was hardly a foregone conclusion. Most marketers would agree that a turnaround could have been effected sooner and at a lower cost, but egos obscured management's view of its problems. Perhaps Xerox was counting on the fictional character that appeared in its ads, the lovable Brother

Dominick, to ask for divine intervention. In the final analysis, they were smart not to wait.

Wrigley's Extra . . . and More

In 1990 the Wm. Wrigley Jr. Company maintained a 48 percent market share of the more than $1.3 billion U.S. chewing gum market—more than double that of its nearest competitor.

"We make two things," a Wrigley executive noted, "chewing gum and money for our stockholders."

That wasn't always the case.

Around 1891, William Wrigley started a chewing gum company while running a baking powder company. A tireless promoter, Wrigley had planned to use the gum as a giveaway to those who bought his baking powder.

He first marketed a brand called Vassar gum to women, adding Juicy Fruit and Wrigley's Spearmint gum to the line in 1893. New start-ups are usually challenging under the best of economic circumstances, but times were tough and it was a shaky beginning for the company financially.

Wrigley had long been regarded as a salesman, a showman, and a marketing genius. He reportedly attributed his ultimate success in business to a lack of fear, adding, "I've been broke three times since I started in business, and it didn't cause me a minute's loss of sleep." At the time of his death in 1932, a little over two years after the stock market crash, Wrigley left an estate worth some $20 million.

He was a risk-taker who borrowed heavily, advertised mightily, and believed passionately in his ideas. He also believed in marketing his products very aggressively.

The company's philosophy a century or so later was to be much more conservative but still highly aggressive.

Already leading the field with its Spearmint, Doublemint, Juicy Fruit, and Big Red chewing gums, the company chose to pass up entering the candy and mint segments of the confectionery market, though some marketers thought such an extension would have been logical and lucrative. Perhaps William Wrigley, grandson of the founder, recalled the attempt by managers of the Life Savers brand to expand the tremendous popularity of their candy-with-a-hole by introducing Life Savers Gum, a very costly and embarrassing failure. Another attempt at extension, Gummy Life Savers, proved weak in test markets and never realized the potential that should have come with the power of that brand.

The Wrigley marketing philosophy was customer driven. The company saw as its mission to "sell the customers what they want to buy, when they want to buy it, where they want to buy it."

With their core products stable and highly profitable, Wrigley marketers looked to the fast-growing sugar-free segment of the chewing gum market, where the American Chicle Group Division of Warner-Lambert was racking up healthy sales with its Trident brand. Wrigley's sugar-free gum, Orbit, rolled out strong and was building fast when a negative product safety report found an ingredient in Orbit could be hazardous to health. Sales for the fledgling brand collapsed in the United States, though elsewhere in the world the product continued strong.

Wrigley executives insisted that just getting a product out for the sake of being represented in a category was not their goal. Wrigley group vice president for marketing Ronald O. Cox maintained, "We are probably more judicious than many companies when it comes to line extension. What we try to do is focus on what would be a good product to offer, rather than just react to trends."

Cox added, "We are also very sensitive in certain areas. first, there's the confusion on the part of consumers with so much product out there, and secondly, the trade has to figure out how they're going to stock 12,000 variations of a single product."

Line extensions and brand extensions were familiar territory to Wrigley. The company had done well with them, relying heavily on market research and thinking long term. "We respond to what's important to the consumer, not to reports of 'what's hot,'" noted Cox.

Aware that the 1980s was a time of many instant successes, instant failures, and a fashion for instant gratification, Wrigley maintained a policy that disregarded pressure to rush to market with products it did not believe in.

According to Wrigley marketing executives, line extensions should be designed to broaden the appeal of the brand to consumers. Line extensions also create a danger of cannibalization of the brand. A short-term management approach normally gets in the way of long-term considerations, these executives believed.

For example, short-term management ignores the volume of the product in the current year's pipeline, takes a "worry about it next year" attitude, and focuses concern on the potential of the competition to gain an advantage.

To Wrigley management, the long-term approach was a more viable way to meet consumer needs and prevent switching to competitive brands due to "voids" in the assortment of products offered. The key, they believed, was not to get too greedy and to allow enough time to provide the highest level of quality to product-line extensions.

Cox referred to brand extension as the "buzzword of the '80s," an opinion shared by a number of seasoned marketers. The belief is that one can save advertising and marketing costs by extending a well-known name into new fields. There are numerous examples on both sides as to whether or not it works, but what are the criteria for determining success? Is it sales? Market share? Profits? And under a long-term strategy, what time frame affords a reasonable period of determination?

Wrigley executives believed successful brand extension depends more on the "art" of marketing than on science. They believed, too, that the best approach is based on five considerations:

1. Product quality has to be a competitive plus.
2. Extension areas must be chosen carefully.
3. "Up front logic" doesn't always work.
4. Brand extensions can't be viewed as "marketing cost-saving efforts."
5. Beware of design firms selling brand-extension scams by putting the brand name and logo on a product that no experience or research tells you is likely to succeed.

This approach seems to have worked well for Wrigley. While the success of competitor Trident may have contributed to the timing of their introduction of Orbit (and later Wrigley's Extra), market research was already steering the company in that direction.

Wrigley's Extra grew from a 5 percent market share to 40 percent of the sugar-free chewing gum segment in seven years. But an even bigger story than the line introduction of a sugar-free gum may well be the introduction of a new flavor, Winterfresh. With the line already represented with traditional favorite flavors (spearmint, peppermint, and cinnamon), new Winterfresh was touted as a breath freshener, as well as a chewing gum.

One report had nervous marketers pitching the idea to Wrigley, pointing out that there was previously no such flavor as Winterfresh among chewing gums, mints, or candies, making this a potentially risky introduction. Wrigley's response was to remind people that there was no such thing as Doublemint until they invented it, named it, and made it a success.

Winterfresh Wrigley's Extra not only was a huge and early success, but, as a trademarked Wrigley property, would be a new extension to the company's Freedent line of chewing gums (offering consumers the pleasure of chewing gum that won't stick to dentures).

Advertising Age has noted that "sugared gums got a sales boost from the 25 cent, 5-stick packs and the 10-unit multipacks. The Wrigley company credits that 'value pricing' with producing the U.S. volume increase."

Part of Wrigley's strategy has long been to increase the market for chewing gum, not just to serve the markets that existed. In the words of one Wrigley executive, "If a consumer has one pack of gum in his or her pocket or purse, he or she will consume that pack of gum. But if we can get more sticks and more packs into the pocket or purse, the result will be more chewing gum consumed." Increasing consumption was addressed by an ad campaign that urged smokers to chew gum when they found themselves in designated nonsmoking buildings and areas. The campaign's theme was that Wrigley's Spearmint gum is the smoker's alternative.

While persons attempting to quit smoking have been encouraged for years to chew gum, this campaign took the approach of saying, "Don't wait until you quit; start chewing and enjoying the gum now."

Despite a decline in ad spending, Wrigley's Freedent, Wrigley's Extra, and "the smoker's alternative" campaigns, as well as promotion of the core brands, have put the company's more than $125 million annual advertising budget to good use. While being aggressive and conservative at the same time, Wrigley has come a long way from the days when the Doublemint Twins invited consumers to "chew your little troubles away."

Yahoo!—A Search Engine Looks Beyond the Net for Its Brand

The concept of the brand as an identifier becomes even

more important when the product itself is difficult to identify. As commerce stood at the threshold of the twenty-first
century, brands were becoming more synonymous with
images. Ralph Lauren, DKNY, and Gap weren't just purveyors of clothing, they were selling an image. But how
does a company offering access to cyberspace define an
image of itself as distinguished from any other company
offering access to cyberspace? Aren't Internet access services, whether they are called gateways or portals or search
engines, pretty much all alike? Do names like Navigator or
Explorer make any difference?

The answer is a resounding yes . . . and maybe. In a very
young industry, little is etched in stone. Like so much in
Internet technology, both the questions and answers are
evolving and expanding at blinding speed. It is risky to list
the names of the most popular Internet search engines or
what each has to offer because they are each changing so
rapidly that casualties, combinations, and redefining are
inevitable. Industry analysts predict that, in the tradition
of automakers, TV networks, accounting firms, and film
studios, only a handful will survive or, at least, dominate
the field. Along the way, names such as Snap! and Lycos
and Infosearch may be head-to-head with Netscape, Excite,
Microsoft, America Online (AOL), and the early front-run-
ner Yahoo!, or they may be partners with any or all of them.

Without getting into the rapidly changing characteristics of each individual service or which giant may ultimately rule, by creating or offering the most super of
search engines, let's remain focused on the *brand* aspect of
the product, as fluid as the product might be at any time.

Clearly, AOL and Microsoft begin with an edge because
of their corporate brand awareness, but whether their
products in this arena will ultimately dominate remains to
be determined. Candy bars and cars are good examples of
traditional products that test, refine, and roll out to achieve
success and market share and with it an opportunity to
savor that success, perhaps even rest on it awhile. But

Fragrances have been introduced to suggest many things—flowers, fruit, a sea breeze, spice—but a *cigar*? Yes, a cigar, as in *Cigar Aficionado*, a magazine that has become as synonymous with "the good life" as with the tobacco product from which it derives its name. Note the elegantly dressed film star on the book's cover and the fine pen resting on the fine leather wallet. This brand is selling a quality of life, and the fragrance is the flavor of the month.

Cigar Aficionado name and logo are trademarks of M. Shanken Communications, Inc. Copyright © 1997 Licensed by The Rainmaker Group.

technology is an area where sudden twists and changes are so common that news of even an *idea* advanced by an unknown upstart company is often enough to send an industry leader's stock price tumbling.

And search engines are nothing but technology.

In the field of search engines, Yahoo! is regarded as first among equals, especially in its early success in brand identification. The most successful pure Internet company, Yahoo! began in 1994 as the brainchild of two Stanford University graduate students, went public in 1996, and by mid-1998 was valued at more than $5 billion and growing, its potential yet to be realized. As the number of Internet users continues to grow and more advertisers become comfortable with the Internet as a mature and viable advertising medium, search services are projected to be critically important factors.

Yahoo! was among the first to recognize this fact and began advertising itself in the traditional and familiar media, using network TV spots and print ads in national magazines. The company also designated a resident brand marketer who arranged deals to put the Yahoo! name and logo on skis, backpacks, shirts, toys, and golf balls, as well as on such innovative venues as Visa cards, the lids of cartons of Ben & Jerry's ice cream, and the Zamboni machine that cleans the ice between periods of the San Jose, California, hockey team's home games.

It has become routine for a brand to put its logo on products unrelated to its own industry, but Yahoo! ironically found a successful branding venture in a magazine sold at newsstands and through mail-order subscription. The product of an industry that positioned itself as an alternative to TV and printed matter was using all of these options to aggressively promote and distinguish its brand from other Internet search engines.

The magazine *Yahoo! Internet Life* was launched in 1995 and, by 1999, claimed a very respectable 600,000 rate base and an estimated four million readers. One of

Just as a recession was about to hit Beverly Hills, Starbucks launched its chain of coffee bars. Across America customers were talking about "that yuppie coffee that was strong at $3 per cup and almost as much again for a brownie to go with it." But the real question of taste was in the lifestyle image the Starbucks customer was embracing. As the brand's sales rocketed, then seemed to level off, the company came out with a somewhat modified Starbucks coffee in supermarkets and introduced granola bars, biscotti, coffee-flavored ice cream treats, and even CDs with music to help create the mood to go with the taste. The brand's managers seemed to understand from the beginning that they were selling more than coffee. The holiday-timed literacy program for underprivileged children struck just the right note with the brand's target demographic group and the magazine, *Joe*, filled in more information between sips of coffee.

Photograph of Starbucks products by Karin Gottschalk Marconi.

more than two dozen Internet magazines to enter the field, *Yahoo! Internet Life* became one of the most successful in terms of advertising revenue and audience acceptance. Typical magazine covers featured Elvis, Seinfeld, or model Cindy Crawford (thereby demonstrating a clear understanding of its target audience), as well as carried

Who says financial advertising has to be dry, stiff, or boring? fidelity boasted the top mutual fund for years. When its manager, Peter Lynch, stepped down from running the fund, the company wanted to maintain its identification with the man credited with so much of its success. He became the self-conscious spokesman for fidelity in a series of awkward ads. The idea of having him act as a straight man for comic performers such as Lily Tomlin and Don Rickles seemed to lose the focus of who exactly Lynch was and what the product was and why they were so good together. Comedy in ads about managing people's money is, to a lot of consumers, a risky business.

Fidelity Brokerage Services, Inc. 1998.

Figure-skating star Ekaterina Gordeeva is the embodiment of performer-as-brand: a beautiful young woman whose skating partner-husband died suddenly, leaving her with a small child and half a career. first there was a book, then a video, followed by a made-for-TV movie, TV specials, interviews, and . . . Katia, the scent. The ad campaign that used as many as 12 photographs in a two-page spread was very light on copy: "She captured your heart. The fragrance that captures Katia." Delicate, subtle, hopeful. The lady had become a brand, and it was only the beginning of a well-orchestrated campaign for personal care products that, if carefully managed, could go on to any number of other Katia branded products.

Katia products are made by Dayton Hudson Corporation. Copyright © 1998 DHC.

ads for Altoids, Calvin Klein, and Marlboro, in addition to those of Apple Computer, Intel, Gateway, and Compaq.

Would the magazine have been as successful if it had been called *Internet Life* instead of *Yahoo! Internet Life*? Very likely not. This is an example of a recognizable Internet name supporting an Internet magazine and the magazine, in turn, successfully promoting the search service. Yahoo! understood the value of its franchise through brand extension possibilities outside its domain, even in a medium that might have appeared to be a competitor. As Microsoft and NBC found an apparent synergy in creating the MSNBC cable TV network, Yahoo! recognized its stock multiple requires that its future be based on something more than the uncertainties of the market for Internet search engines. Yahoo! appeared to have learned the value of a well-positioned, well-publicized brand name. As fashion designers found that a brand name often exceeded the value of its core product when it was licensed to fragrances, furnishings, and other products, Yahoo! found it could extend its reach and value by publicizing its imprint, if only through traditional means of advertising and public relations—and through the most traditional of media. Its potential is greater as a marketable brand than as any single product.

SECTION 3

Creating, Managing, and Marketing Brand Equity

6

A Crash Course in Brand Marketing

In the film *Nothing in Common,* a successful young ad agency creative director is about to drive his father to the hospital in his new Jeep. His father looks upon the vehicle with disdain, at its lack of elegance and style. He mutters, "When are you going to get a real car?"

His son immediately fires back, "This is a real car. *I look good in this car.*"

There you have it—the essence of the results of advertising and marketing. He liked how he *looked* in the car.

What he meant, of course, was that he *felt* good in the car because it represented an image he wanted to step into and wrap around himself: the young ad man in his Jeep—hip, smooth, clever, successful, out of the mainstream, on his way, on his way up.

The right car.

The right watch.

The right wine.

One does not adopt, aspire, or wrap oneself in an image defined by generic products. Brands reflect an image, a personality. Brands help distinguish and define the best in the products we choose and the reasons we choose them.

The marketer who attempts to build a brand on the basis of price alone may get a sale or two but will most likely lose the customer to the next brand that advertises a lower price.

Brand loyalty is based in part on quality, price, service, and image—the elements that constitute value in the mind of the consumer.

Brand equity is the value in and of the brand.

To create, manage, and market brand equity

1. *Use research.* Know all you can about both the pluses and minuses of your own product or service and those of your competitors—past, current, and potential. Know what your customers want and how much they are willing to pay for it. Know to what degree service and quality are important considerations. Keep in mind that everyone says that they *want* service and quality, but will they pay for it? Research can minimize the potential for costly mistakes. Use research seriously, to determine your customers' likes and dislikes. Tuning out customer feedback can be fatal to business.

2. *Use your marketing plan.* Too often marketing plans are developed to impress the CEO or a board of directors. They are presented and accepted, then languish in a file drawer. Marketing success is not dumb luck. A good marketing plan should be like a map, carefully drawn, showing how to get from one point to another with shortcuts included. Your plan should include a situation analysis, objectives, a strategy and tactics, a budget, and a timeline with

benchmarks to evaluate the success of the plan or the need to modify it to reflect changes or unforeseen conditions.

3. *Define the core brand's position clearly.* Remember the old commercial that showed the couple arguing about whether Certs was a candy mint or a breath mint? For arrogance or just a lack of energy, don't let someone else position your product. What is it? Who is it for? What are its strengths and weaknesses, alone and relative to the competition? What is your product or company's image or reputation? Are they such that you can build on them, exploit them, or do they need to be changed in order to give the product or service a fair chance competitively?

4. *Qualify your plan.* Who are your customers (men, women, teens, seniors, a particular ethnic group, generations, working mothers, etc.)? Does your core product meet the needs of one or all your target market segments? Should you consider a brand extension to meet the needs and/or desires of a specific market segment? Will doing so (or not doing so) cost you market share, or will it cannibalize the market for the core product?

5. *Define the value of your core product.* Value is price, quality, and image. Is your product price competitive with that of other brands? If higher, is the value clear enough to justify the extra cost? If lower, does that lessen the perceived value of your product? What is the perception of your product's level of quality, alone and relative to that of your competition? Is your image well defined? Consider the impression that is left by lines such as "For those who think young," "The choice of a new generation," "I'd rather fight than switch," "We bring good things to life," "Nature's most perfect food," "You deserve a break today," or "Where America shops." A product

without a defined image suggests its appeal is to no one in particular.

6. *Consider brand extension as adding value.* A good product doing well should be supported, not tampered with. But when the pulse of the market indicates a need or a desire for something more or something else, consider a companion product with its own defined value, such as sugar-free, sodium-free, fat-free, recyclable, biodegradable, no cholesterol, no additives, etc.

7. *Have a reason for a brand extension.* Often a brand extension is a "competitive counterpunch." Let your research tell you there is a need and/or a desire for the brand extension. Bringing something out just because a competitor did it is risky and expensive.

8. *Define primary and secondary goals.* A primary goal is usually (or should be) generating sales or revenue. Is your product goal market dominance? The support of a social issue or cause? Be clear about if and how goals of your core product and brand extension compete or complement each other.

9. *Don't neglect public relations.* PR is often dismissed as a perfunctory process of sending out news releases that announce promotions of people or events, just to get some press attention. Newsletters, hot lines, surveys, studies, event sponsorships, educational grants, subsidies of the arts, educational texts/audios/videos, and guest columns or editorials can help define the personality of a company or a brand. Consider the impact of the General Electric 24-hour service hot line, the CitiBank 24-hour hot line, the Mobil Oil corporation grant to public television, sponsorship of the U.S. Olympic Team—these are all examples of public relations efforts or programs that influence consumers and regulators, positioning a brand name as a good corporate citizen of the community and

someone nice to do business with. Do not under-
estimate the power, ability to influence, and
effectiveness of a good public relations effort.

10. *Advertise.* Yes, it can be expensive, but if done right,
advertising is much more of an investment than an
expense. Control the space, the content, and where,
how, and how often it is presented can have a very
powerful influence on the impression left behind. It
is essential to successful brand building. It is not a
coincidence that the largest, most successful brands
in the world are also the largest advertisers. They do
it because it works. Several times each year, television
networks present prime-time specials featuring the
best or the funniest commercials of the year or the
decade, and audiences sit through an hour, watching
intently as entertainment the very commercials they
tell market research people that they hate the most
about TV. Some of the best-known, strongest brands
became part of the culture with the classic identifiers
that advertising created: the Marlboro Man and
(Wendy's) "Where's the beef?" "A Kodak moment"
and (McDonald's) "You deserve a break today."
When a brand takes its advertising seriously, even if
the ads are funny, and it *connects with its audience,* it
creates attention, recognition, awareness, loyalty, and
an image that transcends mere advertising to become
part of our individual and collective consciousness.
Consider the brands whose image and market share
collapsed when they heavily cut back or stopped
advertising.

11. *Recognize that promotions are tricky.* They should be
used to create recognition and to help build brand
loyalty, not exclusively for "trial" or discounting.
Sweepstakes can help get attention and, more important, help build a solid-gold database. But they can
also shift attention away from the brand and the

product, upstaging it with hard acts to top, such as trips to Hawaii or Disney World or other glamorous prizes. Try to make a promotion relate to the product, such as AT&T or MCI offering members of the military or students free phone calls home on Sunday, a major oil company sponsoring an energy-saver promotion, or Campbell Soup Company sponsoring a recipe contest. Laws and regulations governing contests and promotions have caused as much as 20 percent of the ad space to be devoted to detailing restrictions, limitations, and disclaimers. When consumers become more interested in the promotion than the product, it does not add up to a long-term successful program for the brand. Good promotions, such as frequent flyer or frequent diner points or discounts and rebates, are sensible and effective because they keep the focus on the brand.

12. *Remember the USP—the unique selling proposition.* This basic rule of advertising and marketing is very often overlooked in favor of "creative" glitz or dazzle. The USP is to provide the consumer with both a reason to buy and a way to distinguish the brand from its competition. Your core brand should have a unique selling proposition, and any and all brand extensions should each have *its own* unique selling proposition— not just exist because there is a core product. What is sillier than seeing an ad that tells you it is for TPW company, a division of IOC Corporation? Who cares? What's the payoff for the customer? Be unique, but remember who is ultimately paying for this, and make certain that they understand *why* they are paying for it.

13. *Don't expand your line solely to look bigger.* Bigger isn't always better. There are limits to shelf, storage, and display space. There is also frequently confusion among consumers about the proliferation of products

and brands. Competition is healthy, but there are limits to what people will accept. The existence of hundreds of brands of cigarettes is difficult to justify, particularly when the category leader may have a market share of 25 to 50 percent. How unique can so many brands be from one another? Focus on creating and managing the equity of your brand, its intrinsic value, and let your extensions be logical, appropriate, and market-wise, not just product explosions.

14. *Be honest and ethical.* When a company invests its talent, energy, and resources in creating value for its brand name, it is then good business sense to protect the integrity of the brand. Lawsuits and corporate crises can tarnish a brand's image (often unfairly), but an open, candid, and swift response can retain or restore trust. American Express, one of the best names in its industry, has been the subject of several scathing, but well-documented, books that reveal a heavy-handed, unethical underside of the company that could only be effectively addressed by having its CEO resign. Sears, Roebuck & Company's automotive center fraud cases, credit division manipulations, store closings, layoffs, and frequent miscalculations have served to promote an image of a management that is out of touch, possibly inept. The Exxon Valdez oil spill is a classic case of corporate arrogance as a response to an environmental tragedy. A respected oil company and a fine brand name will be forever linked with a dark headline that put the brand into eternal disrepute with conservationists around the world. These giant companies could have turned their crises into potential opportunities to do good and, in the process, add luster to their brand names. A pattern of public honesty and ethical corporate behavior creates a reservoir of goodwill from which a company

can draw in times of crisis. Don't exceed credibility in what you promise. That's only good business sense and good business ethics. Projecting a positive image in the long run costs less than projecting a negative one.

15. *Be careful with attack ads and comparisons.* This was a bold idea born of the 1980s, and many marketers would like to believe its time has passed. When civility gives way to an aggressive, confrontational, "in-your-face" style of advertising, one company fires the first shot (usually not the category leader, believing it has little to lose), and rather than taking the high road, competitors respond by trying to "one-up" the attacker. Long-distance phone companies brought this tactic to ludicrous levels in the 1990s. Ads in which one brand attacks another often backfire by giving the competitor a higher level of attention, name recognition, interest, and perhaps even sympathy. The best ads emphasize the benefits of the product advertised. If the best you can say about your product is something negative about your competitor's, your product doesn't have much going for it. Take the high road. Be positive.

16. *Include a promise with your product.* Whether the focus is on your core product or a brand extension, give consumers a reason to buy what you're selling and t o support your brand. Stress the benefits. Add value. Remove real or potential irritants. Create a climate of acceptance. Stand for something your customers and potential customers can align with. Ben & Jerry's ice cream costs more than many of its competitors' products. Its high quality notwithstanding, people support the brand because the company allocates a percentage of its profits to groups working to save the rain forests, promote environmentalism, and other noble causes. So does actor Paul Newman's

company, Newman's Own, as it manufactures and markets salad dressing, popcorn, sauces, and ice cream. Your promise will help set you apart from competitors. Think price, quality, value, and your USP. Add a little something extra that will make customers want to support your brand and cheer for you to succeed. It may help take you a long way.

17. *If you can, be first. If you can't be first, be better.* This point is pretty self-explanatory. The marketplace rewards imagination and innovation. Being original gets noticed. Being first earns the status accorded pioneers and trailblazers, as well as provides advantages that come with being the probable market leader, at least for a while. But if you can't be first, be better. The market doesn't really *need* another toothpaste, cola, or cigarette brand. Make your product stand for something by its benefits, directly or indirectly, to consumers and the community at large. Remember the USP, whether you are the first one out of the gate or the last.

18. *Listen.* David Kearns, the former CEO of Xerox, said the company ran into big trouble when it stopped listening to its customers. Al Ries and Jack Trout offer that "success often leads to arrogance and arrogance to failure." An observation that has been offered before is worth repeating: *There are those who listen and those who wait to talk. Bless the listeners.* We can learn a lot from observing and being receptive to comments and suggestions. If just a little of what's said is worth hearing, the intelligent marketer will recognize its worth.

7

Brand Marketing: Today and Tomorrow

Consumers care about the workings of business more than ever before. There's more business news on TV and radio, and entire cable television stations are devoted to only business news. Solid publications such as *Forbes, Fortune, Business Week,* and the *Wall Street Journal* have been joined by the very successful *Smart Money, Worth,* and *Investor's Business Daily,* in an era where print journalism had been pronounced dead. Corporate CEOs, publishers, network and studio chiefs, and entrepreneurs are the cover subjects of *People* and *Newsweek* and guests on the Barbara Walters TV interviews.

The takeover of RJR Nabisco was the subject of the best-selling book and major motion picture *Barbarians at the Gate.*

With such high-profile corporate posturing comes both an upside and a downside. The upside is greater visibility and the recognition of a broader audience of potential supporters, customers, and shareholders. The downside is that similar mass audiences learn immediately about boycotts, news of failing products, product liability suits, and "green mail."

When Nestlé was the target of a worldwide boycott stemming from its marketing of infant formula to third world countries, the nightly news told of the boycott and its effect on Nestlé units from its candy bars and restaurants to its hotels.

If there was ever such a thing as "spin control," manipulating media coverage to create a specific impression or opinion, it's over. Instant communications allow the public to see and hear directly much of what was once filtered through publicists and editors. Marketers in the twenty-first century must not only understand this, but learn to use it and even to exploit it.

In my earlier book, *Getting the Best from Your Ad Agency*, I predicted that ad clutter would continue to annoy consumers, merchandising would become a more important part of the marketing mix, a smaller percentage of the marketing budget would be assigned to market research, and cable TV would be responsible for changes in the way marketers market and consumers respond. By 1999 NBC and its cable stations CNBC and MSNBC were aggressively cross-promoting programs and branded merchandise, as well as directing viewers to an interactive website.

Ad clutter continues to make it hard for an advertiser's message to be noticed, and harder still for it to be believed. There is a myriad of sincerely represented claims with little or no credibility. The "tune-out" factor is high. Marketing columnist George Lazarus calls this *marketing immunity*. The Pulitzer Prize–winning humor writer Dave Barry has pointed out to his millions of readers, "We have learned to accept that, even though these people have gone to the trouble and expense of buying the advertisements in which they claim they are in the business of fixing things, many of them will not show up . . . I'll tell you what American businesses do a good job of: pretending they care about customers."

Ouch!

Barry's remarks find considerable empathy with consumers who realize that testimonials and endorsements in ads and commercials *are paid for*. The customer satisfaction picture is also pretty bleak. Observers of businesses continue to ask the question, "Why is service so bad?" As yet, no one seems to have come up with an answer. But that hasn't stopped many companies from continuing to suggest that *their* clients are happy, so we must be talking about someone else. Alas, clutter and a lack of credibility go hand in hand. Marketers in the future must, if they can't reduce the clutter, stress the benefits of the product or service to the consumer—the USP (unique selling proposition)—and must not exceed credibility. People will actually try a product that offers a benefit to them, even if it is not equal to the Eighth Wonder of the World.

On the research front, Joe Klein, writing in *Newsweek*, noted that "for the past quarter century, American business has been great at R(esearch), but too impatient to be very good at D(evelopment). It's been left to the Japanese, and others, to take American ideas—like VCRs—and figure out how to manufacture them."

Another problem has been the reluctance of too many companies to invest in research, believing that it would only tell them things they already know. Hence, like so many ad budgets, dollars allocated for research have been cut. Unfortunately, it is the level of corporate arrogance that has not been reduced to a level where common sense can prevail. Research tells you what you need to know about your product, company, competition, and strengths and weaknesses in the marketplace. Advertising presents your image and your message in the best possible terms, the greatest number of times, to the people who need to see it. A reluctance to invest in these key areas and a cautious approach lacking in imagination seems to be guiding business. Note that some highly successful ventures were launched in what many described as "the worst possible time." Success has always grown from commitment.

On the subject of research, "New Product Pacesetters '98," a study conducted by Information Resources Inc., concluded that "Advertising doesn't boost package-goods brands as much as new products do." Maybe so. Listening to the voice of the market means *responding* as well, and if that response is a product that didn't exist before, that's a new product opportunity well exploited. However, if the voice of the market is saying the product that meets consumers' needs is the product you have already brought out, the need may be for more or better brand marketing or promotion rather than for more product.

And on the cable TV front? With long-range plans getting shorter and the promise of 500 channels (keep that remote handy), TV is becoming more like magazines, having a dedicated channel for the most narrow, specific, and esoteric tastes (science, nature, comedy, history, art, weather, foreign languages, medicine, law, and much more).

The dominance of the big TV networks has eroded, and emphasis in the future will be increasingly on niche programming. This will provide highly targeted avenues of opportunities for advertisers and marketing.

Looking Ahead

The ever-rising cost of health care and prescription drugs has increased interest in generic drugs. Pharmaceutical companies, in a move to counter this trend, have positioned ads in major weekly news magazines, similar to those normally run in the trade press, encouraging consumers to become more familiar with prescription drugs by their brand names. These ads, in four-color printing on high-gloss paper, with information normally provided only to doctors, were designed to encourage patients to ask their doctors to consider treating them with specific brand name drugs:

- The ad for the nicotine patch Habitrol carried the pre-headline "No one believed I would ever really quit smoking." A brief testimonial then followed.

- Another bold, colorful ad in the same national magazine carried essentially the same pitch for Nicotrol.

- Still another patch pitch, for Nicoderm, told the same story to the same audience in the same national medium.

- The national news magazine four-color ads for Cardizem CD invite the patient to "ask your doctor if Cardizem is right for you" and call for a free quarterly newsletter on healthy living.

- Norplant System has run color spreads in national news weeklies, attempting to sell consumers on Levonorgestrel implants as a birth-control method.

- Certainly, Viagra must be called a "wonder drug." Because of what it promises, it became the subject of constant conversation, both public and private, and became a household word overnight.

An idea that marketers have been trying to sell for years is *interactive*. It is an idea that had matured by 1998. Phone companies and retailers have joined together in the past with banks and utilities. Home shopping networks brought the concept a bit of show business sizzle. Inevitably, one day, almost everything a consumer could want will be viewed, ordered, and paid for by a techno-hybrid of TV/phone/computer. Cocooning will look more like hibernation, as people never leave home.

The increasing popularity and rapid growth of the Internet and the World Wide Web present new advertising

As generic drugs are increasingly a choice of many cost-conscious doctors, patients and insurance plans, pharmaceutical companies are presenting messages suggesting a quality of life synonymous with the quality of a brand-name drug—urging the marketplace to demand the drug of choice by its brand name.

Viagra ad, copyright 1998 Pfizer Inc.

and marketing opportunities every day. Every business, organization, association, agency, product, politician, and celebrity has a home page or website. These locations are opportunities to display the brand or to subdivide and cross-reference brand information or promotions.

As time goes on, expect more creative initiatives to be advanced. Certainly, as specialization has always been popular, creative directors, artists, and graphics professionals will focus on designing and using personal computers and the Internet field to present and promote brand data.

The trade magazine *Advertising Age* noted this growing area of specialization, reporting, "As online marketing grows in budget size and business importance, interactive agency reviews are growing beyond in-house searches and word-of-mouth recommendations. Traditional consultants are seeing a burgeoning business in handling searches for marketers' interactive needs."

Adweek added, "More—and bigger—advertisers are deciding the Internet is a good place to put their money." The publication reported, "Online (and offline) advertiser dollars will shift to the virtual equivalent of in-store advertising."

There is no way to accurately reflect or predict the future of marketing on the Internet, as the scope and focus of it change day by day. The Internet will be another "avenue of media" as well as another vehicle. Like most tools, it will be used more or less effectively and to a greater and lesser degree, client by client, brand by brand, and with varying success levels. It should be given due consideration in determining what percentage of a given audience can be measured or influenced by its inclusion.

Videos, sold or rented for home viewing, will be thick with brand messages (read: "commercials"), both blatant (ads before and after the featured content) or discreetly (product placements within the presentation).

As shopping carts, service station gas pumps, in-flight locations, bank automatic teller machines, waiting rooms, and public restrooms have all become placement positions for advertising, coming up with new and creative venues will continue to present challenges to marketers.

No presentation on the future of brand marketing should overlook the Earth. That is to say, the public continues to have a maturing appreciation for products and brands that are both safe and good for the environment. These "green" products carry labels attesting to their safety and purity. Being good for the environment is certainly good in and of itself, but it is also a device that encourages brand loyalty and respect. If consumers believe a brand marketer is sincere in the commitment to environmental issues, no discounts, coupons, or smooth talk is likely to lure them away.

Since the concept of selling came into being, it is safe to conclude that *trust* has been a factor in how people decided who they'd do business with. Thus, the idea of "brand names" gained in importance. And a trusted brand name on a new product borrows against the established trust to get a trial and evaluation. As trends come and go, the trusted names tend to survive.

Successes achieved by new market entrants at the expense of established brands may cause some to question whether or not the very concept of brand loyalty is out of date. One possibility is that trends and business itself can be cyclical. In a tough economy, interest increases in generic brands, representing lower-priced items, only to be replaced during an economic upswing by a desire for products with a higher level of quality and image—a brand name.

Private labels and house brands are on the rise. But as manufacturers add words like *premium, gold, choice, special, gourmet, limited,* or even *private label* itself, and charge prices comparable to name brands, ultimately the name brand wins out. Rarely do private label products enjoy a level of promotions comparable to that of brand names, so they rarely enjoy the same level of loyalty that comes from the familiarity of a name.

Crain Communications executive and former publisher of *Advertising Age* Joe Cappo notes that increasingly, retailers have gone from being the distributors of brands to showcasing their own private labels. In some cases, such as that of The Gap stores, their own exclusively. On clothing and other select items, the names Bloomingdale's, Marshall Field's, Tiffany, Neiman-Marcus, and others are every bit as much leading, desirable *brand* names as the brand names they once featured. In the future, there will be greater recognition, acceptance, and broadening of this practice. Retailers, investing heavily in raising their profiles, sharpening their images, and taking advantage of that imagery with heavily promoted private label brands, will further blur the lines between retailers and the products they sell.

Finally, the sentiment was echoed earlier that the personal computer is in its infancy. It has been for several years and continues to stay young with each new advance in technology. The Internet and the World Wide Web became virtually "overnight sensations" as everyone and anyone seemed to have a website or a home page. Everyone means the Library of Congress to the used-book shop around the corner. While retailers, service providers, and individuals post electronic addresses and invite the world to "visit," the jury is still out on how marketers will most effectively put this system to use.

Home shopping, chatting, and amassing information continue to be expanded and refined at the consumer level. The loss of personal contact will itself provide a further marketing opportunity. Businesses will increasingly find this technology an alternative to printing sales literature and catalogs, maintaining showrooms, and supporting an army of sales reps. In simplest terms, the new technology is a new medium; the marketers who master the use of this medium will realize advantages that previous generations found in newspapers, magazines, radio, television, direct mail, and out-of-home media.

It may take some time to fine-tune the machinery at the consumer level, but on a business-to-business basis, Internet technology has produced an efficient, effective means to present, display, and promote the brand, its extensions, and its possibilities.

Brands will be around as long as the marketers of brands keep their fingers on the pulse of the marketplace . . . and that pulse can quicken rapidly.

Bibliography and References

Aaker, David. *Managing Brand Equity.* New York: Free Press, 1991.

Advertising Age, Special: "100 Leading National Advertisers," September 23, 1992.

———. "Coke II Spot Goes Flat on Persuasion." September 7, 1992.

———. "They're Back!" January 11, 1993.

Adweek, Special: "Superbrands: The Most Powerful Brands in the World." 1990.

Alsop, Ronald, and Bill Abrams, eds. *The Wall Street Journal on Marketing.* New York: Dow Jones & Company, 1986.

Barry, Dave. *Dave Barry Does Japan.* New York: Random House, 1992.

Beckwith, Harry. *Selling the Invisible.* New York: Warner Books, 1997.

Beirne, Mike. "Crispy Cruncher." *Brandweek.* September 14, 1998.

Boyd, Harper W., and Robert M. Clewitt. *Contemporary American Marketing*. Burr Ridge, IL: Irwin Publishers, 1962.

Business Week, "Rethinking IDS from the Bottom Up," February 8, 1993.

Cappo, Joe. *FutureScope: Success Strategies for the 1990s and Beyond*. Chicago: Longman Financial Press, 1990.

Clark, Eric. *The Want Makers*. New York: Viking Press, 1988.

Cote, Kenneth. "David Kearns: How I Saved the Titanic." *Fortune*. January 1992.

Delaney Report. "Time Management." February 16, 1992.

Donaton, Scott. "Playboy Expands to Custom Titles." *Advertising Age*. May 18, 1992.

Egan, Timothy, "The Swoon of the Swoosh." *New York Times Magazine*. September 13, 1998.

Elliott, Stuart. "Billion Here, Billion There . . . ." *New York Times*. June 24, 1998.

Enrico, Roger, and Jesse Kornbluth. *The Other Guy Blinked: How Pepsi Won the Cola Wars*. New York: Bantam Books, 1986.

Fahey, Alison. "Coke II Sneaks into Cola Combat Zone." *Advertising Age*. May 11, 1992.

Gates, Bill. *The Road Ahead*. New York: Viking, 1995.

Gershman, Michael. *Getting It Right the Second Time*. San Francisco: Addison-Wesley Publishing, 1990.

Hafner, Katie. "After Windows 98: The Future According to Microsoft." *New York Times*. May 21, 1998.

Hambleton, Ronald. *The Branding of America*. New York: Yankee Books, 1987.

Harmon, Amy. "A Goliath Needs the Little Guys: Microsoft Faces Challenge of Image Among Consumers." *New York Times*. May 19, 1998.

Harris, Thomas L. *The Marketer's Guide to Public Relations*. New York: John Wiley & Sons, 1991.

Harvey, Richard D. "Why Cola Growth Is Stalling in Food Stores." *Advertising Age*. June 22, 1992.

Hays, Constance L. "Campbell Soup Hopes a New Campaign . . . " *New York Times.* May 20, 1998.

————. "No More Brand X." *New York Times.* June 12, 1998.

Hisrich, Robert D. *Marketing.* New York: Barron's, 1990.

Hwang, Suien L. "RJR Sees Its Cigarette Sales Recovering." *Wall Street Journal.* May 14, 1992.

Jones, John Philip. *What's in a Name? Advertising and the Concept of Brands.* New York: Lexington Books, 1986.

Kearns, David T., and David Nadler. *Prophets in the Dark.* New York: Harper Business, 1992.

Klein, Joe. "Clinton's Project Addiction." *Newsweek.* March 22, 1993.

Krol, Carol. "Yahoo! Internet Life Finds Real Success in Virtual World." *Advertising Age.* March 8, 1999.

Lazarus, George, and Bruce Wexler. *Marketing Immunity: Breaking Through Customer Resistance.* Burr Ridge, IL: Dow Jones Irwin, 1988.

Levy, Steven. "Focus on Technology." *Newsweek.* May 25, 1998.

Liesse, Julie. "Brand Extensions Take Center Stage." *Advertising Age.* March 8, 1983.

————. "Brands in Trouble." *Advertising Age.* December 2, 1991.

Lohr, Steve. "Microsoft Fight Will Be Waged on Wide Front." *New York Times.* May 20, 1998.

Mand, Adrienne. "Acting Up." *Adweek.* September 14, 1998.

Marconi, Joe. *Beyond Branding.* Chicago: Probus Publishing/ McGraw Hill, 1993.

————. *Crisis Marketing: When Bad Things Happen to Good Companies.* Lincolnwood (Chicago): NTC Business Books, 1997.

————. *Getting the Best from Your Ad Agency.* Chicago: Probus Publishing/McGraw Hill, 1991.

Mitroff, Ian, and Thierry Panchant. *We're So Big and Powerful Nothing Bad Can Happen to Us.* New York: Birch Lane Press, 1990.

Ourusoff, Alexandra, Paul B. Brown, and Jason Starr. "What's in a Name?" *Financial World*. September 1, 1992.

Perman, Stacy. "Attention K Martha Shoppers," *Time*. October 6, 1997.

Pogrebin, Robin. "Master of Her Own Destiny: For Martha Stewart, a One-Woman Show with Many Flourishes." *New York Times*. February 8, 1998.

Pollack, Judann. "New Products Top Ads in Helping Brands Grow." *Advertising Age*. May 11, 1998.

———. "RJR Takes Brazen Tone in New Camel Campaign." *Advertising Age*. May 11, 1998.

Poole, Claire. "Marketing Moocher." *Forbes*. September 1, 1992.

Ries, Al, and Jack Trout. *Positioning: The Battle for Your Mind*. New York: McGraw Hill, 1986.

———. *The 22 Immutable Laws of Marketing*. New York: Harper Business, 1993.

Rutherford, Andrea C. "Candy Firms Roll Out 'Healthy' Sweets, but Snackers May Soon Sour on the Product." *Wall Street Journal*. August 10, 1992.

Schlossberg, Edwin. *Interactive Excellence*. New York: Ballantine Publishing Group, 1998.

Snyder, Beth, and Alice Z. Cuneo. "Consultants Tap Market for Web Agency Searches." September 14, 1998.

Solomon, Jolie. "When Cool Goes Cold." *Newsweek*. March 30, 1998.

Tedlow, Richard S. *New and Improved*. New York: Basic Books, 1990.

Torres, Craig. "Fading Brand-Name Loyalty Might Sway Investors." *Wall Street Journal*. April 6, 1993.

Vanity Fair. "The New Establishment (Bill Gates)." October 1998.

Winters, Patricia. "Pepsi Max Sweetens Diet Cola Stakes." *Advertising Age*. March 8, 1993.

Wirth Fellman, Michelle. "Personal Touch, Omnipresent Company." *Marketing News*. March 30, 1998.

Index

About the Author

Joe Marconi is a marketing communications consultant and writer with more than two decades of award-winning advertising, public relations, and marketing programs to his credit. He has been both a corporate communications executive and principal of a major national agency.

Marconi is a frequent lecturer and marketing communications seminar leader throughout the United States and Canada. His writing has appeared in numerous publications, including the *International Herald Tribune,* the *Chicago Tribune, Marketing News,* and *American Demographics* magazine. He is the author of six previous books: *Getting the Best from Your Ad Agency; Beyond Branding; Shock Marketing; Advertising, Influence, and Family Values; Image Marketing; Crisis Marketing: When Bad Things Happen to Good Companies;* and *The Complete Guide to Publicity: Maximize Visibility for Your Product, Service, or Organization.* He is also the editor of *The Marketing Communiations Executive Summary,* a twice-monthly newsletter. Joe lives in Western Springs, Illinois, near Chicago.

The American Marketing Association is the world's largest and most comprehensive professional association of marketers. With over 45,000 members, the AMA has more than 500 chapters throughout North America. The AMA publishes nine major marketing publications and sponsors 25 major conferences per year, covering topics ranging from the latest trends in customer satisfaction measurement to business-to-business and service marketing, attitude research and sales promotion.